ROADMAP

TO RETIREMENT SECURITY

How to Build and Conserve Retirement Wealth

STEPHEN BUTLER

OPEN BOOK
EDITIONS
A Berrett–Koehler Partner

ROADMAP TO RETIREMENT SECURITY
HOW TO BUILD AND CONSERVE RETIREMENT WEALTH

iUniverse books may be ordered through booksellers or by contacting:

iUniverse
1663 Liberty Drive
Bloomington, IN 47403
www.iuniverse.com
1-800-Authors (1-800-288-4677)

ISBN: 978-1-4917-2058-5 (sc)
ISBN: 978-1-4917-2059-2 (e)

Printed in the United States of America.

iUniverse rev. date: 01/20/2014

Contents

Part 1—Building Financial Security

Introduction

This book provides what people need to know about investing from start to finish from the day they sign up for their first retirement plan until the day, on their deathbed, they give away what's left of what they own. It is divided into two parts that cover distinctively different activities. The first part is devoted to building retirement assets, while the second focuses on how to invest in a way that may preserve the nest egg for a lifetime.

Until recently, the average American's most valuable asset was the equity in his or her home. Today, it is the value of their retirement account, primarily their company-sponsored retirement plan and/or their collection of individual retirement accounts (IRAs) that derived from company-sponsored retirement plan rollover money. In addition to that major source of wealth, however, many people have other money that they have saved, inherited, or generated by the sale of a home or business. Investing money in any retirement plan is easier because of the tax-free treatment of these dollars. Investing other taxable assets can be an entirely different challenge. This book focuses primarily on retirement fund money for the same reason Willie Sutton robbed banks. It's where the money is. However, a later chapter does address the challenges of investing taxable money and offers advice about how to invest one's way through the minefield of investment taxation that can otherwise rob from our successes.

This book describes the guiding principles that have traditionally led employees to retirement-plan investment success and financial independence. It offers advice covering the entire spectrum of what people need to know, regardless of where they are in the retirement-investment process. From the young employees signing up for their first plans to someone actually spending his or her retirement plan money in retirement, the book offers a "track to run on," including simple illustrations of investment concepts. The mysteries of the investment world will fade away in the face of these clear teaching tools. Moreover, the book is designed to be an inspirational answer to those of you who claim, "We just can't deal with it." This book is for you more than anyone else.

The first chapter outlines why the voluntary retirement plan (401(k) or 403(b)), a powerful and flexible financial tool, has allowed Americans to accomplish so much since its invention more than thirty years ago. The next chapter outlines the most basic fundamentals of investing, followed by a discussion of the basic asset classes: stocks, bonds, and cash. Then there's an explanation of what mutual funds are really all about. The next several chapters address how to make sense of the different funds and the extent to which they can be combined successfully. Learn how professional investors increase their rates of return while reducing their level of risk. And finally, once you've made a pile of retirement money, how do you shift gears and start spending it without running out? That's the question explored in part 2 of this book.

I have been designing, installing, administering, advising, and improving 401(k) plans and other retirement plans for over thirty years. A major part of my effort has been educating employee participants. For more than sixteen years, my weekly financial column in fifteen San Francisco Bay area newspapers has offered a steady stream of investment basics that have helped readers capitalize on positive economic forces while avoiding human behavioral failures. Understanding the system and avoiding mistakes increases the potential for reaching retirement goals.

The first 401(k) plan my company ever installed was at a San Francisco company in 1980. In January 2010, at the company's annual retirement-plan employee meeting, a person who had been in this plan for thirty years said, "Steve, I took your advice. I stayed the course (mostly in stocks) while the markets were falling apart, and now I'm back up to $2.5 million."

This person had deposited an average contribution over the years of about $10,000 per year. The total for thirty years was $300,000. Since roughly one-third of that $10,000 each year was "paid" with money that would have otherwise disappeared in taxes, his actual cost in take-home pay was only about $200,000. His average rate of return over the period was a typical 10 percent per year. Voila! He now has more than enough money to retire. He can retire early, in fact.

Today's average 401(k) plan account balance for people over age fifty-five is more than $200,000. This figure is based on government information that includes only retirement-plan accounts. It fails to include retirement-plan money that has long since rolled into individual retirement accounts (IRAs). It's safe to say that the average retiree, when the day comes, has between $300,000 and $1 million in their accounts, and this kind of money can support an adequate retirement income stream when invested wisely.

The *Wall Street Journal* cites the growing number of retirement-plan millionaires, while a McKinsey and Company study points out that the average American worker has five times more in retirement benefits than would have been the case had 401(k) or 403(b) plans not been invented. These successes have been an accident in legislative history; lawmakers never anticipated how effective the programs would be. The old joke about "We're the government and we're here to help" actually turns out to be true in this case.

You Don't Have to Wait until Retirement

Our voluntary retirement plan has proven to be history's most powerful financial tool for accomplishing the financial goals sought by most of us as working Americans. Buying homes, educating children, saving for emergencies, and providing for our retirement are the primary reasons we save. While retirement plans are designed to provide financial security in retirement, they can be extremely valuable resources for meeting financial goals before then. The loan provision offered by most plans, the financial hardship provisions, and the access to cash while between jobs can play major roles in the ongoing financial security of all working adults. Long before retirement itself, the purchase of homes, funding of education, and a variety of other financial goals can be met by accessing retirement-plan savings.

I'll share a real-life example. Recently, a newly reemployed middle-aged participant was eager to sign up for the maximum annual contribution to his retirement plan. In the course of our conversation, he mentioned that tapping his previous retirement-plan account while between jobs had been the key to keeping his home and his family together. Given this person's firsthand experience of the value of a financial lifeline offered by the retirement plan, he needed nothing to convince him to replenish his account with maximum contributions. After all, the retirement plan is currently Americans' most powerful tool for accumulating meaningful amounts of money.

What's the Secret to This Savings Phenomenon?

The government's sanction, or "invention," of tax-deferred retirement plans effectively amounts to a substantial government subsidy. Why? Because our voluntary contributions to the plan come right off the top of our pay, before any taxes are calculated. Some of what we would otherwise have paid in taxes is, instead, deposited into our retirement-plan accounts. Then, as the money starts compounding (money earning 7.2 percent doubles every ten years), all of our earnings on assets accumulate tax free. When we combine this subsidy of tax savings with our employer's willingness to offer the convenience of an automatic payroll deduction (and maybe even a matching or profit-sharing contribution), we can see why most people say that their retirement plan is their only long-term savings plan that has ever worked.

But Then You Get to Spend the Money

At retirement, the accumulation phase ends and supporting a lifestyle begins.

For many people, this is more challenging (if not just plain scary). By comparison, the steady building of assets over the years with the help of your employer was easy. Now, everybody wants to help you manage what has become a significant account balance. But you're now alone with your money. Acting on bad advice can cost half of what you've saved over the years.

Nobody but you has interests that are 100 percent aligned with yours. The nicest people in the world can rationalize what's in their self-interest, and nowhere is this more pronounced and misplaced than in the financial services industry. Part II of this book will lead you in the right direction and help you understand the basics of generating the income you need while avoiding the risk of losing your nest egg.

How the Book Is Structured

The purpose of this book is to help you understand the basics of investing in light of the unique characteristics and framework of your retirement plan.

The topics we will discuss are presented in the following order:

Chapter 1—Set Your Goals and Wake Up Rich

You need to know what you're trying to accomplish before you can structure a cohesive investment plan.

Chapter 2—The Fundamentals of Risk, Return, and Time

It never hurts for even sophisticated investors to recall that risk and return are related and that time reduces risk. The temptation to think short term is the hobgoblin at all levels of experience.

Chapter 3—Three Asset Classes: Cash, Bonds, and Stocks

What we can expect of each and how they work together to increase returns while reducing risk. How, for instance, do bond investments actually work?

Chapter 4—Mutual Funds

The investment medium of choice for retirement plans and the world's most profitable industry at our expense. What a mutual fund is and how we can get the most from them.

Chapter 5—More on Stocks (How They Work)

Since stocks play the dominant role in helping us reach long-term retirement goals and help maintain adequate retirement income, we need to appreciate the underlying reasons for their value and fully understand events that would otherwise shake our confidence in this most valuable investment tool.

Chapter 6—Adopting the Cornerstones of Intelligent Investing

How we use investment building blocks to begin crafting a strategy for success.

Chapter 7—The Automatic Pilots of Retirement-Plan Investing

Once we have a strategy in place, how we keep it from getting derailed. What we need to know about economics and financial market history to bulletproof our asset-building efforts.

Chapter 8—Choosing Your Investment Mix

The final step in managing your retirement plan is to pick the investment mix. What investment choices make the most sense based on your goals and your comfort level with risk?

Chapter 9—Managing Other Money

Many people have "after-tax" money saved outside their retirement accounts. Managing this money requires the application of tax-saving investment techniques, because every investment decision is impacted by potential income tax costs.

Chapter 10—The End Game

This is a lead-in to part 2 of the book—the section that teaches us how to effectively "flip the switch" from the period of building assets to one of generating income to support retirement lifestyles. How we can arrange our investments so that we maximize our income but don't run out of money.

Part 2—How to Live a Life and Not Outlive Retirement Resources

Chapter 11—Introduction

A general glimpse into the future for someone at the threshold of retirement.

Chapter 12—Show Me the Money

An overview of where money will come from and what to expect in income from retirement resources.

Chapter 13—Where to Take Your Money

It may come as a surprise to learn that the last place to take your retirement money is to most of the huge financial institutions that want desperately to offer their assistance.

Chapter 14—A Case Study of Retirement Finance

This chapter offers a real-life example of how a couple might structure their lifestyle and investment mix to generate adequate income and not eat into their principal.

Chapter 15—The Danger Zone

This is a cautionary note as to what can happen if too much money is removed from the nest egg early in the retirement years.

Chapter 16—Taking Your Money Out

This chapter outlines the sources of money that you will be choosing to access and which ones should be turned to first.

Chapter 17—Using a Financial Planner

The temptation to financial affairs over to a financial advisor can be great for many people, but the expense is considerable and the advice may be self-serving—for them. This chapter offers some guidance as to how to sort through the planning/advice universe and create a constructive relationship—if you need one at all.

Chapter 18—Test-Driving Your Retirement

Cutting the cord to a professional life and career can be traumatic. When at all possible, it can make sense to do it gradually. At the same time, you can organize your financial affairs over time so that the shock of retirement is less intense. This chapter offers some valuable suggestions and thoughts on retirement beyond just those related to investing.

Why This Book Is So Important

The level of success you achieve as a retirement-plan participant depends more on the skills you develop as an investor than on the amount of money you sacrifice each pay period. You can work hard or you can "work smartly." It's best to do both, of course, but the purpose of this book is to help you develop the skills needed to "work smartly" as you develop what will be a retirement-plan fortune.

The financial basics and investment techniques outlined in the following pages will help you understand the history and the mysteries of the investment world. This information will guide you to greater success over the years ahead.

Chapter 1—Set Your Goals and Wake Up Rich

The *Wall Street Journal* published an article titled "Waking Up Rich—Retirement Accounts Stashed in Stocks Make Employees Millionaires." The article's author stated, "The retirement plan rich are changing their lives. Quitting jobs early, taking extended holidays, starting new careers—or restructuring jobs to make them more fun." These retirement-plan millionaires are people who never thought of themselves as having any personal wealth and suddenly they realize that they do. They are feeling good about it.

Another interesting insight for the article was this: "For some people who thought they wanted to retire early, having a financial cushion has a curious effect ... for many people the security of a nest egg allows them to relax and enjoy work more."

Today, many people approaching retirement have had an opportunity to participate in a 401(k) plan for the past thirty years. The first plans were rolled out in the early 1980s, and almost all major companies adopted them immediately. Even most small companies offered some retirement-plan opportunity, even if they could not afford an employer matching contribution.

Most people who have been contributing for this entire thirty-year period have somewhere between $300,000 and $1 million in a combination of their current, company-sponsored retirement plan and the rollover IRA account (or accounts) formed as they changed jobs over the years.

If these numbers sound high, consider the example of someone who earned $40,000 a year back in 1980 and who saw steady increases in pay until reaching $70,000 a year today. These are rough average pay levels for American workers over this period. At an average contribution level of 6 percent of pay per year (the nation's average retirement-plan voluntary contribution), and assuming an average rate of return of 10 percent per year, this typical employee would have accumulated just over $500,000.

In most cases, the employer has been contributing at least some amount of additional money over and above the voluntary contribution from the employee, so the total percentage contribution would have been higher than 6 percent of pay. Moreover, the average mutual fund through the

'80s and '90s actually increased in value at a rate of more than 15 percent per year instead of the 10 percent historical average stock-market return used in our calculation above. Factor in these reasons for improved results, and we can see why a $1 million account balance is within reach for many people.

The underlying facts speak for themselves. Today $3 trillion is invested in 401(k) plans, and an estimated $3 trillion more is invested in rollover IRA accounts resulting from previous retirement-plan contributions. The total amount in all mutual funds today is $9 trillion, so we can assume that two-thirds of that figure is attributable to the 401(k) plan phenomenon.

If you're young, with thirty years of work ahead of you, those numbers should be inspirational. If you're older and partway up the ladder, you can assess what course correcting, if any, you may want to do to reach your intended goal. If you're close to retirement and these numbers seem unreal or certainly not applicable to you, then you have made one or more of three mistakes along the way.

1. You're not committed enough to saving.
2. You've spent big chunks of what should have been rollovers when you left your job.
3. Or you've made some bad investment decisions.

The purpose of this book, regardless of your retirement-plan stage in life, is to provide you with the tools you need to make constructive, informed decisions that will help you reach your goals.

Identifying Goals: An Important Consideration for an Investor

Let's start with Warren Buffett, who says, "You shouldn't buy any stock that you're not prepared to hold for ten years." In the meantime, the stock market can be volatile for reasons having little to do with the intrinsic value of the companies in which our mutual funds have invested. When J. P. Morgan was asked what he thought the stock market would do, he answered, "It will fluctuate."

To invest intelligently then, we need to understand the following: a fundamental cornerstone of investment decision-making is the time frame or length of time that the money can be committed to an investment.

Without a clear understanding of our goals, it is impossible to know for certain how much time we are allowing an investment to meet our expectations.

There Can Be Confusion about the Time Frame of Goals

For young people, a common misconception is that the company-sponsored retirement plan is exclusively for retirement savings and that their only investment goal is long term, thirty-five to forty years. In fact, younger employees can often have short-term goals for portions of their retirement-plan money, thanks to the fact that retirement-plan loans offer access to what is generally long-term retirement money. Down payments on homes, educational expenses, and many other financial objectives short of retirement can be reasons for using the retirement plan, since the pretax dollars make this the fastest way to accumulate wealth.

The Young Are Different …

Younger people are also different in that their lives are in flux. This means that they can expect to be unemployed from time to time until they get settled in a career. Between jobs, it's not a sin to tap retirement-plan accounts to pay for rent and food. Moreover, retirement-plan money can be a source of support while taking a year or more to go back to school.

There are extremely important reasons, well short of retirement, to be saving money. There is no more powerful savings "machine" than a 401(k) or 403(b) plan with automatic payroll deductions, tax savings, and even employer matching contributions in many cases. Any young person who would rather not move back in with parents or live on a friend's couch, should jump at the chance to sock away some retirement-plan money. Anyone who has an occasion to tap this lifeline will never again have any doubts about the value of the retirement-plan opportunity when settled in a future job.

If my spouse and I are in our thirties, both contributing the maximum, can we retire at age fifty?

Relatively young people have been able to retire in recent years long before what is normally considered to be retirement age. This doesn't mean they quit working altogether. But more important, they have been able to consider career options for reasons other than earning enough to support their lifestyles.

Two spouses contributing an annual $10,000 each will have a total of $1 million in twenty years if their investments earn an average of 10 percent per year, the stock market's average annual return. That $20,000 total contribution for a two-income couple costs their family unit about $13,000 in take-home pay.

It's that simple.

If we're in our fifties now, aren't we within ten or so years of our goal of retirement?

Ten years to retirement may be true, but if you are in good health and have parents who lived long lives, there is a possibility that you will need money for many years. While retirement itself is just around the corner, a portion of your retirement money is still subject to a long-term goal.

Someone fifty years old today may still need their money to be growing at age eighty-five, the same thirty-year time frame that a thirty-year-old employee is considering.

Here's a formula that some investment advisors suggest: divide your age by one hundred, and that will indicate what percentage of your assets you should have in bonds. Does age sixty-five over one hundred indicate that 65 percent of your money should be in bonds and 35 percent in stocks? Hold on a minute. That won't work for someone who might reasonably live to age ninety, and it ignores the equity someone may have in their home. Home equity amounts to a combination of a stock and a bond. (It's more like a bond.) These common formulas that define many package retirement investments (target or lifestyle funds) are much too simplistic for most situations.

The information in this book will arm the retirement-plan participant with a broader understanding of what they need to know to better meet their retirement goals.

We talked about young people, but what if any of us lose our jobs?

Is retirement the only reason for retirement-plan savings? Who knows? Many of us are employed in volatile industries that periodically subject us to layoffs and extended periods of unemployment. This might be the most effective reason to be building a nest egg, our retirement plan. Between jobs, we can tap this money at any time and use it as our personal unemployment compensation. While the money is taxed just like job income, plus a 10 percent penalty for anyone younger than fifty-nine and a half, receiving it in a year when little or no work has reduced income may mean that the only "tax" will be the penalty itself. Moreover, there are no social security or Medicare taxes (8.5 percent) on what would be distributions from a rollover IRA, so this helps soften the blow of the penalty. Later, back at work at the next job, anyone who has experienced the "lifesaver" that the retirement plan represents will need little convincing to participate with the highest voluntary contribution possible.

Investment Decisions Start with Identifying Goals

Goal-Setting Exercise
Write down all the reasons you can think of for why you would want to save money.

- one- to five-year goals
- ten-year goals
- twenty-year goals
- thirty-year or longer goals

The longer a goal, the greater the boost from the "invisible hand" of economic forces.
The reason goal setting is so important is because investments offering more volatility will outperform more stable investment types. If we clearly identify a longer period for some of our retirement money, we can be comfortable with the risks that will yield a higher return over time.

While the overall stock-market yields an average of 10 percent per year, small companies grow on average at a rate of 12.5 percent per year. What's it worth to take the risk of investing in them? On a $10,000 annual investment, the small stocks will be worth an extra $200,000 in just twenty years ($572,000 versus $763,000).

The longer a goal, the less a financial crisis matters.
The collapse of stock prices in 2008 and early 2009 was in response to a failure of the financial services industry, primarily the banks who had made and packaged bad loans. So what? The time before that, the market crash was due to the bursting of the Internet "bubble." Before that, in 1987, it was the invention and then the failure of "programmed trading," where computers newly introduced for investment management all freaked out and decided to sell at the same time.

The great thing about these temporary disasters is that the market always recovers. They're only a problem for someone with a short-term goal who has to sell everything in the middle of the crisis or someone who just can't handle what is only a big loss on paper. A long-term goal kept in mind throughout is what allows us to just shrug off these market downdrafts. We can sleep like babies.

It may further help to realize that market crashes often coincide with a reduction in the size of the economy, which leads to recession and joblessness. But remember this fact: the average recession lasts only sixteen months, and while the unemployment rate increases, the remaining people still working tend to receive, on average, pay raises of about 3 percent. The stock market can be completely disconnected from an economic engine that may have slowed down, but that engine is still producing a huge amount of output. Think about this: the stock market dropped in value by 50 percent during 2008 and early 2009. Do you think that the total value of America's public companies and their economic output dropped by that much overnight?

Of course not.

Also, we have to remember that most market crashes follow a previous high-yielding "blowout" of increased stock prices that left investors giddy. The temptation is always to compare where we are after the crash with that unreasonable (we might say "undeserved") high-water mark that our account balance hit at the height back when we all felt like geniuses. If we compare where we are at the bottom of a crash to a time further back like five or ten years, things are never all that bad and we're clearly making progress.

With Goals Established, We Can Move on to the Basics

Investment success rests with understanding the relationship among risk, return, and time. The next section explores how these three investment components, like a three-legged stool, work together to create the wind under the wings of investment performance.

Chapter 2—The Fundamentals of Risk, Return, and Time

1. Risk—a self-assessment of risk-taking ability
2. Return—an appreciation of what higher returns can accomplish
3. Time—the time frame of goals

Keeping the fundamentals uppermost in mind will be a key factor in the successful outcome of retirement-plan investing over time.

The man who knows more about risk, return, and time than anyone else in the United States is Warren Buffett, our second-richest citizen. Here is some advice from his book, *The Warren Buffett Way*:

"Fear and greed move stock prices above and below a company's intrinsic value. In the long run, the value of stock holdings is determined by the underlying economic business; not by the daily stock market quotations."

"If you expect to purchase stocks throughout your life, you should welcome price declines as a way to add stocks more cheaply to your position."

"The future is never clear. What we know today is that there are well-managed companies that consistently make money, and the stock market values them periodically at foolishly high or low values."

Buffett recognizes that he is neither richer nor poorer because of the market's short-term fluctuations in price, since his holding period is longer term. As Buffett puts it, he would not care if the stock market closed for ten years; it closes every Saturday and Sunday and that has not bothered him yet.

How do we apply the same wisdom to our retirement-plan money?

We need to first understand the basics: risk, return, and time are the three "engines" driving our financial success as we begin to match our goals and objectives with the investments offered in our retirement plan.

Risk

Risk is a measure of the possibility that we might lose money.

The most obvious loss of money is an actual reduction in our account balance during what might be a bad quarter (or bad year) for our investments. This experience will always be difficult for us, even when we know the loss will be only temporary.

Fear of the unknown is always lurking somewhere in the back of our minds. We're thinking, *This time, it's different. This time it really is doomsday!*

The key words above are "fear of the unknown." The more we educate ourselves about investments and how they accomplish their miracles, the less the fear factor will influence our thinking. (The less it will "mess with our heads.")

As President Roosevelt once said, "All we have to fear is fear itself." The underpinnings of risk have more to do with emotion than rational thought. Fortunately, there are some mathematical measurements of risk that can satisfy anyone looking for more than the random "casino atmosphere" offered by stock markets in general.

When investing in stocks, there are two types of risks. The first is the risk that a single company or companies in the same industry may suffer a loss of sales, profits, and value. The second is that the entire stock market may be under assault by the herd mentality of people who want to sell in a panic.

Eggs in More Than One Basket

The first risk can be alleviated by spreading investments over several different types of companies and industries. This is called *diversification* or *diversifying*. Most mutual funds own as many as two hundred different companies, so while one company might get into financial trouble, the chance of all of them failing is too remote to bother seriously considering. Then most mutual funds specialize in investing in a certain type of company (large companies, small companies, foreign companies, etc.). While one type of company may be having trouble, other types will be thriving. We reduce risk by dividing our funds among different types of mutual funds. (Diversification is discussed again later in the book.)

Stock-Market Crashes Lead to Economic Strength

The second risk is alleviated by just knowing that stock markets have the capability to "snap back." Since 1970, there have been seven major market crashes with between 25 percent and 50 percent losses. On average, we have seen a rise by 39 percent the first year following a crash and 12 percent the second year. (More on this later when we discuss how to make money on these downdrafts.) Apart from the crashes, there have been many "corrections." These are "mini-crashes" that occur while the market is generally rising, and they can freak us out because we think that each one is the beginning of another major crash. The mini-crashes last, on average, only about a month before the market gains resume. In stock-market history, there has never been a 365-day period that did not have at least one correction of 10 percent or more.

As mentioned in the previous chapter, the average recession, which usually prompts a stock-market decline, lasts only sixteen months. Many stock-market crashes and "corrections" actually take place during strong periods in the overall economy. We'll look at this disconnect again later in the book.

Other Types of Risk

Bonds and money-market funds also involve risk, even though we are taught to think that money is safe (or safer) in these investments than it would be if it was invested in stocks. The risk is more subtle but can be just as destructive as a stock-market crash, which we will see as we learn about different types of investments.

Inflation, the Hidden Cost of Taking No Risk

A more subtle form of risk is the inflation that eats away at the value of our retirement accounts. As time goes by, the goods and services we buy become more expensive by a few percentage points per year. Those few percentage points of inflation tend to be mirrored, year after year, by the rate of return on money-market funds or savings accounts. The rate of return on money that involves no risk tends to be just about same as the annual rate of inflation. Therefore, while cash reserves may seem to be making money each year and offer the guarantee of never experiencing a year of losses, they offer no gains beyond the rate of inflation.

If someone promised to pay us $1,000 per month for the rest of our lives, in twenty years, that $1,000 would be worth only $400 in today's dollars, assuming the inflation rate was 4 percent per year during that time. Another way of putting it would be to say that if you could buy a full tank of gas today, you'd only be able to afford a 40 percent fill-up twenty years from now with that same amount of money. And this example assumes just 4 percent. In the early 1980s, inflation for a few years was at 18 percent per year.

Return

Investors receive a return when they own something or loan something. We own something when we invest in stocks. We loan something when we choose funds that invest in bonds. Even money-market funds are a form of bond investment, although the "loans" are for very short periods (in many cases, just a few months) and they are called "notes" instead of "bonds." Making loans in the context of your retirement plan means choosing an investment that invests in bonds or notes.

Owning something in the context of your retirement plan means selecting an investment choice (a mutual fund) that invests in shares of stocks in different companies. When you own stock in a company, your stock represents an ownership share in a business.

Any business that makes a profit is free to apply those profits in one or a combination of the following ways:

1. It can pay them out to owners each year in what are called dividends.
2. It can reinvest them back into the company to increase the company's size and value so that owners can sell the company itself in future years for more than they originally invested. In the stock market, the rising price of the stock from day to day represents the recognition that profits are being made, first of all, and that they are being reinvested to create more business value.

In the end, whether your retirement-plan investments are in stocks, bonds, or a combination of both, your return will consist of the following:

Yield
The amount of dividends or interest paid by the stocks and bonds your mutual funds have chosen as investments. This money, paid out either monthly or every six months, is automatically reinvested by purchasing additional mutual-fund shares. In retirement plans, because money can't be removed from the plan until after age fifty-nine and a half, the earnings on stocks or bonds are always automatically reinvested.

Total Annual Return
This is the increased value of your account starting with the yield and adding to it any increase in value of the stocks and bonds your mutual funds own. The total increase in value of all these sources will constitute the total annual return of your retirement-plan account balance.

The relationship among risk, return, and time?
Why is risk worth taking? Because people who can endure more risk can expect a higher return as long as they have given themselves enough time to recover from periodic market meltdowns.

During the past fifty years, the market has dropped at least 10 percent more than forty times. No doubt about it, the market will fluctuate. The following matrix illustrates the amazing degree to which risk takers, however, can be rewarded over time.

$10,000 per year investment

Rate of Return	10 Years	20 Years	30 Years	40 Years
2.5%	$112,034	$255,447	$439,027	$674,026
5.0%	$125,779	$330,660	$664,388	$1,207,998
7.5%	$141,471	$433,047	$1,033,994	$2,272,565
10.0%	$159,374	$572,750	$1,644,940	$4,425,926
12.5%	$179,786	$763,608	$2,659,464	$8,815,920
15.0%	$203,037	$1,024,436	$4,347,451	$17,790,903

These numbers are all linear. For a $5,000 annual investment, just reduce the above figures by half. For $20,000 per year, they should be doubled, etc.

Time

Of the three "engines," time is by far the most important. This is why nailing down goals and the time they will require is a critical step in the investment decision-making process.

Time is to investing what oil is to engines.

We can see from dramatically increasing numbers that accepting some risk will increase returns. Why does more risk yield higher returns over time? Because of human nature, a group of people who want to invest money where it will generate the highest possible returns will have to turn to high-risk investments. So-called "venture capital" offers the highest risk of any investment type; less than one out of ten ventures ever pay off. However, when that one out of ten hits big, the profits can be enormous.

As retirement-plan investors, we can take risks that will increase our returns and yet not experience a prolonged loss of money. Economic history proves that time reduces the risk of losing money in stock-oriented mutual funds.

The following chart illustrates the power of time in its ability to iron out the volatility of rising and falling markets. This visually illustrates that with rolling ten-year periods, an investor in the

American stock market would have had almost no ten-year period of losses. In other words, since 1929, any stock-market investment spread across all the stocks sold in the stock market would have earned a positive return if left for ten years.

Rolling 10 Year Returns

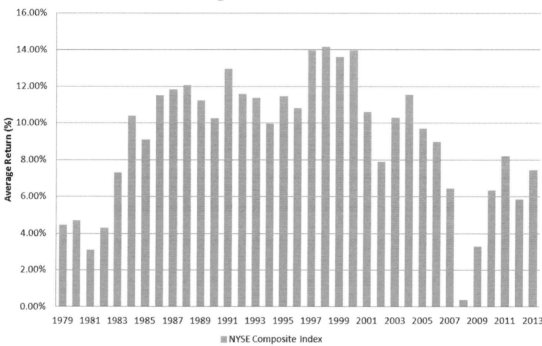

American Return (%)

NYSE Composite Index

(Note: What looks like almost no return or a misprint for the year 2009 is due to the fact that the average rate of return for ten years ending in 2009 was a small fraction of 1 percent. That year marked the end of what has been called "the lost decade.")

Understanding the relationships among risk, return, and time is a critical component of any hope for success as an investor. A thorough appreciation for these fundamentals provides the basis for a more "set-it-and-forget-it" or an "automatic pilot" approach to investing, which leads to the best results over a long period.

Let the markets do the heavy lifting. Getting rich is easier than you think.

Unfortunately, it's sometimes dangerous when we start to think. While the average mutual fund increased in value at a rate of 15 percent per year from 1985 through 1999, the average mutual-fund investor gained only 3 percent. Why? Because the average investor chased the previous year's best-performing investments. Or they switched in and out of the market at the wrong times.

Terrible investment results are only a symptom; the actual disease is a lack of understanding of the fundamentals: risk, return, and time.

The next key to the vault of investment knowledge is an understanding of the basic types of investments, the tools we need to *build* financial resources.

Chapter 3—Three Asset Classes: Cash, Bonds, and Stocks

Like the basic food groups, there are three basic categories (or classes) of investment: money-market funds (cash), bonds, and stocks. There are other asset classes, such as real estate and oil, as well as hard assets like gold. However, the vast majority of retirement-plan investments are directed toward the most basic of investment types.

Cash

The advantage of this asset class is that we know we will not lose money and that we are guaranteed to make at least something, however small, in interest each year.

We know, however, that inflation robs our savings of any value gained from interest paid by money-market funds.

Bonds

A bond typically pays a higher rate of interest than cash because bonds are "loans" for longer periods of time. A typical bond might have a maturity of ten years, which means that it amounts to a ten-year loan. Because loans of this length involve more risk (something might go wrong in ten years that we can't anticipate today), interest rates paid on bonds are higher than what the US government would be paying on thirty- to sixty-day notes. A note is just a bond with a very short time period to run before being paid back. This time period is the "maturity" of the bond or note.

So-called "junk bonds" are high-risk bonds (loans) to companies that may not be able to repay the loan. Despite the possibility of losing money, people invest in junk bonds anyway because these bonds pay interest rates that might be as high as 15 percent per year.

The Important Difference between Long-Term Bonds and Cash

While cash involves no risk, the interest rate paid on these very short loans is just about the rate of inflation. The lenders (savers like us) are taking no risk and want to receive only enough interest to keep in line with what would otherwise be the erosion of their money's value caused by inflation. Inflation, remember, is when today's $1 loaf of bread costs $2 five years from now. The bread didn't become more valuable. Instead, the value of the dollar was reduced to half of what it will buy today.

Bonds involve a longer-term commitment, and because of this, they pay higher interest rates than short-term notes. Bond values are priced every day just like stocks, and the total value of the bond market in the United States is four times larger than the total value of the stock market.

It is possible for a collection of bonds to decrease in value even though all their required interest payments are current and there is no indication that the borrowers would be unable to pay the money back. This happens when interest rates in the open market have risen and the original bonds owned in the fund are paying interest at the old original rate.

The value of the existing bonds will go down in a case where they are compared with, or compete with, brand-new bonds that are suddenly offering a higher rate of interest.

By the same mechanism, bond mutual funds can rise in value if interest rates on the open market happen to fall. When market rates fall, those original bonds paying a higher rate are suddenly worth more money if we want to sell them.

We can think of this like a rope over a pulley. One side of the rope represents market interest rates (like the ones we read about when, say, we learn that mortgage rates are decreasing). The other side of the pulley represents the capital value of the bonds.

Let's say we bought a ten-year bond for $1,000 that pays 5 percent interest and will "mature" and pay back the $1,000 in ten years. In the meantime, it will pay us $50 per year, which is the annual interest we earn. If we wanted to sell the bond after just five years, its value would depend on what brand-new bonds were paying in interest. If they were paying only 4 percent, our bond might sell for $1,200 and we would have a $200 profit. But if interest rates in the market were now as high as 6 percent, our bond could be unloaded for only $800, because at this price, our $50 annual interest payment would be equivalent to a 6 percent return. As our bond approaches maturity, when the $1,000 payback is guaranteed, what had been a rise or fall of value in the meantime goes away.

Bond mutual funds, just like stock funds, are valued every business day based on the market value of every single bond in the fund. This means that the entire value of the mutual fund can rise or fall based on interest-rate changes in the bond markets.

Stocks

Stocks are the pieces of paper or certificates that represent someone's ownership interest in a company. By saying, "I own stock in that company," the person has stock certificates or proof of ownership. Over time, the American stock market has yielded rewards that have exceeded those of any other form of investment.

Owning stocks has been a hedge against inflation and is one of the best opportunities for harnessing the "magic" of compound interest.

Owning a share of stock in a company means that we actually own part of that business. A large company can be thought of as a huge pizza, with its ownership divided into as many a twenty million slices. Each slice, known as a share, may sell for $20 today. Tomorrow, however, a share may sell for more or less depending on the demand for that company's shares, specifically, or the demand for shares in general. Someone buying a share today for $20 may be able to sell it tomorrow for $22 (a 10 percent profit), or it may only be saleable for $18 (a 10 percent loss). Looking back over the last one hundred years, stocks have performed by far the best of all the basic investment groups.

The average stock has generated annual returns that are about 7 percent higher than the average rate of return on savings accounts or thirty-day United States Treasury notes.

Individual stocks and bonds are cumbersome to manage and keep track of, so retirement plans typically use mutual funds as the investment vehicle. What exactly are mutual funds and what advantages do they offer investors?

Chapter 4—Mutual Funds

Where can I find an investment advisor I can afford?

If investments in stocks offer the best approach to long-term success in building a retirement nest egg, the average investor needs access to a means of investing that taps into the know-how of seasoned professional investors. Investment managers with proven track records can be compared against each other. To be practical and cost effective, the services of these advisors need to be available with ease and minimal cost. Mutual funds offer the best access to professional investment assistance.

What are mutual funds?

Mutual funds provide the opportunity to invest in a professionally managed investment pool that purchases stocks in hundreds of different companies. As you contribute money into this pool by buying shares in a mutual fund, you are buying a percentage of all the stocks in the pool.

Each business day, the value of the entire pool is calculated based on the price of every share of stock owned by the pool at the end of that day. The total can be hundreds of millions, if not billions, of dollars. *As an investor, you actually own a small percentage of all those stocks. The value of your investment goes up or down on a daily basis as the stocks owned by the pool change in value.* If you want to cash in (redeem shares from) your account, the mutual-fund company sells enough of the stock it owns to generate the cash needed to cover the check they will be sending you on that day.

The advantage of a mutual fund is that it offers the novice or small investor some access to the best investment managers in the world. It also offers *diversification* (discussed in detail below) so that even small amounts of money are spread out over hundreds of different stocks. This reduces risk.

Protection for the investor comes from the fact that the underlying stocks purchased by the fund secure the investment. The investor's account is always worth its proportionate share of all the stocks owned by the fund. Every stock owned by the fund would have to drop to zero in value (bankruptcy) before the mutual fund would lose everything. The collection of stocks and/or bonds in a mutual fund is referred to as the fund's "portfolio."

How do the returns of stock-market mutual funds compare with those of bond funds and money markets?

If you had invested $1,000 in the average stock mutual fund twenty years ago, you would have about $8,000 today, and that period includes two major stock-market crashes. The same $1,000 invested in a money-market fund over the same period would have grown to just $2,000.

That's an amazing difference. How do professional managers do it?

Managers review specific industries and monitor prices of the stocks in those industries. They tap vast resources of data not practically available to the small investor. They monitor, for instance, the buying and selling activity of corporate officers (known as "insider sales"), which is public information by law. They also monitor the macroeconomic environment to determine economic swings and to assess how these major moves in the economy will affect stock prices.

In some cases, a diligent money manager will monitor the activity in the parking lot of a new company to see how many employees are working late at night after business hours. This is seen as a measure of the degree to which the company's success is an obsession of its employees. Obviously, average investors do not have time for this level of hands-on company research; the money investors effectively pay to have mutual-fund managers perform activities such as this is probably money spent in the best possible way.

Diversification: It Helps Us Sleep at Night

A major factor in overall success is diversification. While one stock may prove to be a loser, the gains from others can more than offset that loss. The individual investor would find it impossible to achieve the diversification offered by participation in a mutual fund. One $20 investment in a single mutual-fund share can be spread out over the ownership of hundreds of different companies, creating miniature investments of just a few cents in each company. Our $20 investment would mean that we owned six cents worth of Apple, two cents worth of Coca-Cola, etc., depending on what investments our mutual fund happened to hold.

When a Little Means a Lot

Each additional percentage point of interest earned over time can translate into millions of extra dollars in the future. We would all love to make a killing overnight, but investment success is more often measured in fractions of a percent over long periods.

The following matrix illustrates the extent to which just one more percentage point per year can make a difference. We begin with a common 10 percent example, the difference between earning

9 percent and 10 percent. We also include a 14 percent versus 15 percent example, because there have been twenty-year periods (1980 through 1999) when the stock market has averaged 16 percent per year. The first ten years of the new century have been described as "the lost decade" because stock prices were largely flat. However, some mutual funds gained as much as 14 percent per year during this period.

$10,000 per year contributed over twenty-four pay periods

% Annual Earning	10 Years	20 Years	30 Years
10%	$171,178	$642,491	$1,925,836
9%	$162,568	$566,549	$1,570,441
Value of extra 1%	$8,610	$75,942	$355,395
15%	$232,057	$1,279,641	$6,008,782
14%	$215,656	$1,079,734	$4,541,874
Value of extra 1%	$16,401	$199,907	$1,446,908

The stock market historically has averaged a 7 percent per year better rate of return than money-market funds. Why, then, would anyone with at least twenty years until retirement choose to relegate themselves to a money-market fund at 3 percent versus the stock market at, say, 10 percent?

How do mutual funds make money?
Mutual funds subtract their charges on a daily basis from whatever they may be making as their profit or rate of return for the investor. When a mutual fund's rate of return is expressed in any fund ranking or report to investors, the result is always expressed as "net of fees," which means that the fees have been subtracted before the fund's rate of return was published.

These expenses are what you, as the investor, pay to get the mutual fund to work for you. The charge is deducted automatically from your account on a daily basis and your annual rate of return will be reduced by whatever the management fees add up to. You will never receive a bill or have to write a check for them. They are just automatically collected.

On the previous page, we pointed out how much a difference of 1 percent can make in long-term investment success. While most actively managed funds charge an annual cost of 1 percent per year, index funds charge about 0.2 percent, an 80 percent discount. Some index funds now charge as little as 0.07 percent. (The reason index funds are so cost effective is explained in the next paragraph.)

What are "index funds"? Are they different from mutual funds?

Index funds are mutual funds too, but they are a type of mutual fund that is set on "automatic pilot." This means that there is very little active management of the money along the lines of what was described earlier. Instead, index fund managers buy a broad cross-section of companies that represent a mirror image of the entire stock market or some specific portion of it. After that, no further stock picking or trading is done. For instance, if General Electric represented 5 percent of the country's stock-market value, then an index fund would have 5 percent of its assets invested in General Electric stock. That's it. No hanging around in parking lots to try to determine the stock market's next "winner."

The largest mutual fund in the world, holding almost $150 billion, is the Vanguard 500 Index, a cross-section of the largest five hundred companies in the United States. Each stock owned by the fund is owned in proportion to that company's amount of outstanding stock, in dollars, relative to the total value of the outstanding stock of all five hundred companies. "Outstanding stock" means the amount of stock actually available on stock markets that is owned by investors. About 30 percent of the entire value of the 500 Index consists of the outstanding stock of only fifty companies. In other words, while the index includes five hundred companies, a handful of huge companies dominate the fund's results from day to day.

These largest five hundred companies also make up roughly 70 percent of the entire value of the US stock market. Although there are a total of 6,500 public companies, the remaining 6,000 firms beyond the biggest five hundred amount to only 30 percent of the stock market's total value.

While the 500 Index is the eight-hundred-pound gorilla of the investment world, there are index funds of every stripe that reflect the returns of smaller portions of the stock market. There are more than two hundred different types of index funds ranging from those that invest in small companies to those that invest only in large companies that pay dividends.

The advantage of index funds, and the reason for their popularity, is that they don't cost very much to operate. There are no investment geniuses earning multimillion-dollar annual salaries. There are fewer ongoing trading costs because stocks are not being bought and sold ("churned") in the portfolio.

The theory behind index fund success is that their lower fees and trading costs will more than compensate for the lack of active management. A theory was developed thirty-five years ago by some Stanford professors who threw darts at the stock page of the *Wall Street Journal* and bought the stocks that the darts hit. They proved that buying stocks randomly and then not messing with them (a buy-and-hold strategy) would yield results that would outperform 80 percent of all active efforts to manage money (after the fees and costs had been deducted). The theory holds that 70 percent of any one stock's performance (up or down in value) is a result of what the stock market as a whole is doing. The best and brightest money managers in the world will be looking at a 70 percent probability of losing money if the stock market is headed down. We all want to know which managers will be in that 20 percent group who beat the market, but it is impossible to know who these managers will be. At least some members of the 20 percent club just got lucky.

Meanwhile, the Stanford professors have gone on to win Nobel prizes for discovering the "efficient markets," "random walk," and "wisdom of crowds" theories, which all derived from the dart-throwing experiment. More recently, the hypothesis has been retested using a chimpanzee to pick the stocks. The original results have been confirmed.

What Mutual Funds Accomplish

The mutual-fund concept offers a window of opportunity enabling us to invest small amounts of money in giant pools that have even more economic clout than Bill Gates or Warren Buffett. Armed with this valuable tool, investing can become as easy as learning how to swim or drive a car. It's important to appreciate how just an understanding of the fundamentals will generate better overall investment results than those achieved by others who spend time becoming self-styled investment experts. As Ernest Hemingway once said, "Some intellectuals are the dumbest people I know." The investment world is littered with people who have "lost sight of the forest for the trees." Their investment results have been dragged down by indecision or an effort to be too clever.

Applying basic investment fundamentals is much more important than knowing a lot about company finances or attempting to second-guess what will happen in the stock market or the economy.

All we need for success is to choose an investment mix that offers the maximum returns for the level of risk we can tolerate. As a general rule, the more volatility (higher gains and bigger losses) we can tolerate, the more money we will accumulate in the long run. However, there are some refinements in investment technique that can increase profits without increasing risk. The ideal investment mix incorporates some of these techniques, and the next three chapters will help us identify and use these tools as we select our investment mix.

Chapter 5—More on Stocks: How They Work

How can we have faith in a less-than-perfect system?

How the Stock Market Makes Billionaires of Some and Causes Anxiety in the Rest of Us

Do you ever wonder how a twenty-six year-old Silicon Valley software engineer can become worth a billion dollars seemingly overnight? He or she may have been one of a handful of employees working for what had been the garage-band equivalent of a startup only a few years earlier. It's simple. If a startup gets some traction and sells, say, 50 percent to a venture capitalist for $10 million, the other half owned by the founders, thanks to their sweat equity, is worth the other $10 million. A few years later, perhaps 10 percent of the company is sold for $100 million, which makes the owners of the other 90 percent—the founders and that venture capital company—worth $900 million. And so on. Taking the company public introduces "the greater fool theory" (no matter what I pay today, someone else will pay more tomorrow), thanks to the participation of unsophisticated stockholders. Their frenzied buying creates an inflated multiplier that sends the value of all shares right off the charts. As a general rule, a company that goes public instantly creates a company whose total stock becomes worth four times what its value was deemed to be as a private concern days earlier.

Alternatively, we have recently suffered through the experience of watching the entire stock market plummet by 22 percent in the single month of October 2008 and another 30 percent a few months later. That's nothing. On October 19, 1987, the market lost 27 percent in a single day—not to mention recent "flash crashes" that prompted officials to close trading.

To understand how these extraordinary determinants of wealth—both positive and negative—can take place, we can start with an appreciation for a stock-valuation mechanism referred to as "marked-to-market." It means that all outstanding stock in a company is valued based on the share price of what is being bought and sold at a given time. In the above example, we saw how 10 percent selling for $100 million made the whole company effectively worth $1 billion. For public companies, only a miniscule fraction of their total stock actually sells on Wall Street on a given day—far less than 1 percent. But the sales price of that miniscule percentage sets the price for all the remaining stock in the company.

While this sliver of stock changes hands throughout the day, the last transaction is listed as the day's closing price. That then determines the value of *all* shares of that stock for whoever happens to own it. At day's end, our mutual funds, owning stock in hundreds of companies, will be valued based on the total number of shares and the closing price of each company owned by the fund.

Marked-to-Market

Overall, a system that uses a stock-market sale to determine a value for entire companies may not be a perfect system, but it's the best that we have. To see how imperfect it can be, consider a simplistic application of a marked-to-market mechanism to better understand the concept.

A brand-new home in a housing development, complete with furniture, sells for $100,000. The $100,000 includes a couch that was worth $1,000 or 1 percent of the home purchase price. The new owners put the couch up for sale at the end of the driveway because they just don't like it. A neighbor buys the couch for $500. If the value of the home was "marked-to-market" and 1 percent of the package just sold for $500, then the entire house is suddenly worth $50,000. If the couch had sold for $1,500, the house would have risen in value to $150,000. In other words, the sale price of whatever part of the house was for sale determined the value of the entire house.

Back on Wall Street, the demand for whatever part of the public company is for sale determines the entire value of all outstanding shares in the company. By comparison, a private company with no stock sold on Wall Street can only be valued based on what an outside appraisal (or their banker) thinks the entire company—or some percentage of it—is worth. The true value is what a willing buyer would pay a willing seller for the whole thing or at least a meaningful slice. Unlike a public company, there is no "little sliver" of ownership being bought and sold every day on an open market.

Why did we see such a dramatic, across-the-board plummeting of stock values starting in September 2007 followed by a spectacular "snapback" since then? The culprit? A marked-to-market valuation mechanism. The supply and demand for stocks became disconnected from the intrinsic value of the companies whose value they were, in theory, representing. Actually, the majority of companies in 2008 made higher profits than they did in 2007. Why, in the single month of October 2008, would the entire stock market drop an average of 22 percent? And why would it drop another 30 percent in the first few months of 2009? The supply of stocks that institutions like hedge funds were desperate to sell far exceeded the amount that people wanted to buy—except for Warren Buffett. The Sage of Omaha describes the stock market as a "voting machine" while a company's true worth—its balance sheet—is a "weighing machine."

Warren Buffett has made the bulk of his fortune over the years by recognizing times when the market was suddenly inefficient—when it was suddenly and temporarily no longer an effective measure of the underlying value of companies. This is why, in 2008, Mr. Buffett invested billions in companies like Goldman Sachs and General Electric (and has tripled or quadrupled his investment as a result).

Here it is in Mr. Buffett's own words: "The future is never clear. What we do know today is that there are well-managed companies that consistently make money, and the stock market values them periodically at foolishly high or low values."

Think back to the couch and the house. We know that a house doesn't have huge swings in value based on the sale price of just a piece of it. In business, there can be times when two entirely different prices can apply to the same company. Like an entire house that we know has a basic value, an entire company can have a specific value based on its ability to sell a product and make a profit. Over on the stock market, however, an entirely different value can be established because of an oversupply of stock coupled with a low demand for stock in general.

The Lesson from Our Generation's Very Own Great Crash

The current economic situation presents one of the best views ever into the workings of Wall Street and the basic fundamentals that we depend upon to generate the wealth needed to meet financial goals in retirement. Understanding the occasional disconnect between companies themselves and the stock they have for sale on Wall Street can help us ride out these swings in value.

Of the six major stock-market crashes since 1973–1974, the twelve months after reaching the absolute bottom of the market after each crash saw an average rise of 39 percent. The second twelve months' return averaged 12 percent, and the third year's return was 4 percent. This was just the average of the six crashes. The greater the downdraft, the more substantial the "snapback." Witness the 70 percent gain in just the twelve months following the 50 percent drop ending on March 6, 2009. In the end, the market reverts to the norm. An "invisible hand" of economic forces rewards those who accept some risk and generally pays them an average of 7 percent above the rate of inflation. The long-term rate of inflation has averaged 3 percent. Adding the 7 percent "risk premium" to the 3 percent inflation rate provides us with a total of 10 percent per year—but with, needless to say, some major ups and downs along the way.

Here's some final advice from a great book *The Warren Buffett Way:* "Fear and greed move stock prices above and below a company's intrinsic value. In the long run, the value of stock holdings is determined by the underlying economic progress of the underlying business; not by the daily stock market quotations."

For most retirees, the stock market will be a necessary tool well into their retirement years. The dividend stream provides income and the rising capital value keeps the ravages of inflation at bay. The thought that retirees must hold is that the capital value of their account doesn't matter in the short term. All that counts is the dividend stream, and even during recessions, that stream of income has held up reasonably well.

Chapter 6—Adopting the Cornerstones of Intelligent Investing

The key to a successful investment mix starts with a clear understanding of your objectives and moves to a selection of investments that fits your needs and personality. Since there is no single investment that offers high returns with low risk, your job is to create a mix that meets your desired rate of return at a risk level with which you can live comfortably.

Diversifying or spreading your retirement-plan money across different types of investments can reduce your risk and help create your *path of minimum regret.* In financial circles, this is officially referred to as the *efficient frontier.* It is the point at which you have taken your maximum allowable risk, and your investments are set up to generate the maximum rates of return that can be expected from that risk level.

So much for theory. Which mix of my retirement-plan fund choices will best help me reach my goals?

To determine which fund or combination of funds makes the best sense for you, begin by answering the most basic fundamental question.

"When do I plan to need this money?"

Next, review the investment characteristics of the different types of asset classes (cash, bonds, and stocks) along with their risk/return relationships.

Understand how different asset classes meet the needs of different goal time frames.

Cash

One- to four-year goals. Money-market funds preserve cash. The money will always be there, even though it doesn't earn much in annual profit.

Bonds

Four- to seven-year goals. Bonds can drop in value temporarily, but while they present these capital fluctuations, they will generally earn more than cash.

Stocks

Seven-year-plus goals. Stocks are by far the most profitable of investment classes, but they can lose the most in single years.

Most retirement-plan investing is long term. Even after retiring, people still have years of inflation to contend with, so stocks play a large role well into old age.

Never expect too much from stocks as short-term investments. Remember that 70 percent of any one stock or stock mutual fund's performance is based on what the stock market as a whole is doing. You can have the greatest mutual fund or stock in the world, but if the stock market is dropping in value, there is a 70 percent chance that your great mutual fund (based on past results) will also be dropping in value. This means that if you picked the worst mutual fund available, you would still be doing at least 70 percent as well as the average fund. A falling tide lowers all boats.

Let's combine some economic and investment fundamentals to see how they apply to real-life situations.

First, we need to ask which of these three levels of risk best describes our basic comfort zone.

1. Conservative Investor: "I need to know that my investments are increasing steadily each year. I realize that this psychological or practical requirement will mean lower returns in the long run."
2. Moderate Investor: "I am willing to accept occasional losses knowing that accepting this risk is the price I need to pay for higher returns over time."
3. Aggressive Investor: "I am seeking maximum long-term gains and will not be concerned about short-tem losses."

The following matrix illustrates what we can expect in returns and risk levels from the different percentage combinations of stocks and bonds. These averages are based on the twenty- and thirty-year periods ending in 2010. It may come as a surprise to learn that very similar results are generated using the twenty- and thirty-year time period ending in 1993, nearly two decades ago. That previous period began with the stock-market crash of 1973 to 1974.

Can you share a stock-market statistic that provides some more reassurance?

We have been through seven major stock-market crashes from 1973 to the present. In each case, when we have been able to look back and identify the exact day of the bottom of the market, we find that the average rate of return for the following twelve-month period has been 39 percent. The second twelve-month period following the crash has seen an 12 percent gain. While some of the crashes were more severe than others, these were the averages. The greater the crash, the greater the "snapback." From 2008 until March 2009, the market lost almost 50 percent, the greatest loss since the Great Depression of the 1930s. The most recent snapback, however, has been 180 percent over four and a half years.

While adding bonds to a stock portfolio can blunt the effect of a stock-market crash, they will also reduce what can be expected for a total portfolio return. Review the following matrix carefully, and use this information to develop a sense of what level of short-term "investment pain" you can tolerate in return for longer-term gains.

Investment Mix	20-Year Avg. Return	2002 Loss	Total Return 1/1/2002 to 12/31/2005	Total Return to 2010 over 20 years
100% Stocks	11.10%	-17.21%	72.79%	820%
80% Stocks 20% Bonds	10.23%	-13.75%	63.64%	700%
60% Stocks 40% Bonds	9.35%	-9.64%	53.64%	597%
40% Stocks 60% Bonds	8.47%	-4.66%	42.69%	508%
20% Stocks 80% Bonds	7.60%	1.50%	30.63%	432%
100% Bonds	6.72%	9.30%	17.30%	367%

This chart illustrates that the conservative portfolio of 100 percent bonds lost less and corrected faster, but over twenty years, it accumulated about one-third less money than the 100 percent stock portfolio.

This grid is important to review carefully. Ask yourself how you would feel in a major market downturn. Is it worth it to you to lose 30 percent or more if you stand to have twice the account balance in twenty years? Do you have twenty years left before retirement?

Like the warning on your car's passenger-side rear-view mirror, the actual results may be bigger than they appear. The figures illustrated above are based on broad cross-sections and averages of American stocks and bonds. In an actual retirement-plan investment selection, there will be a variety of investment types that will create more diversity and possibly less risk. A mix of different types of stock-market investments (including, for example, an international fund or small-company fund) will generally reduce the amount of loss in a market downturn while maintaining the same gains that would have been expected of the market as a whole.

To illustrate this last point, the period from 2001 to 2010 has been describes as "the lost decade." This refers to the fact that the broad stock-market averages, even including reinvested dividends, earned almost exactly zero during this troubled time frame. It has been the worst ten-year period in stock-market history. Yet a combination of specific stock types, such as small-company stocks and foreign stocks, has actually earned an average of about 6 to 7 percent per year over that same period. In the following chapters, we'll learn how to combine a mix of these different investment styles to improve results over the long term.

A mix of investment types (diversification) can reduce risk and increase returns. Experiencing how each different style performs during periods of an economic cycle can lead to a practice of selling at least some of today's winners before they become tomorrow's losers and vice versa.

Chapter 7—The Automatic Pilots of Retirement-Plan Investing

What are the differences among different funds, and why do they matter?

Beyond the influence of the stock market itself, the second most important influence on investment success is the investment *style* of the money manager or mutual fund. Mutual-fund managers each adopt different styles of investing. Over extended periods, "Every dog will have its day," in the sense that a particular style will do better than others during a portion of a business cycle.

The key is to have several different dogs in the hunt.

Value investors specialize in large companies that have recognizable value in the form of, say, cash, factories, or brand recognition. Warren Buffett is the classic example of a value-oriented investor; he says he looks for companies that have relatively little debt, consistent profits, and what he calls a "moat" around them that makes it difficult for other companies to compete.

Growth investors invest in growing companies that borrow as much money as they can and that reinvest every dime of their profits. They hire more people, lease more space, and buy more capital equipment as fast as possible in an effort to grow their share of their market as quickly as possible.

Blend is just what the name implies—a mutual fund that invests in companies that include both value- and growth-oriented companies.

All three of these approaches can be applied to *large, medium,* and *small* companies, so we wind up with a *style box* that we can use to identify the style of the investment.

	Value	Blend	Growth
Large			
Medium			
Small			

When this nine-frame box is used to describe a manager's style, one of the boxes will be filled in to indicate where the manager's mutual fund fits.

In addition to these basic styles, we can also have funds with styles best described as "out of the box." This refers to different types of mutual funds beyond just the style definitions. These different types would be, for example, foreign funds or industry-specific funds, such as technology, precious metals, health care, emerging markets, real estate, and many other subcategories of investment types.

Also out of the box would be bond funds that are buying loans rather than owning stock in companies. Bond funds also have their own style box, which identifies the level of risk and the average maturity of the bonds they hold.

Why is style and/or investment type important?

We are always moving through economic cycles. (See explanation below.) They never stop. *At any point during an economic cycle, one or two style combinations will be winners over all others.* A year or so later, during a different period of the cycle, another style combination will be on top. Just about the time we are reading that small companies and technology companies are "hot," we will begin to see a period when those investment types start falling out of favor. Instead, large "blue-chip" companies paying generous dividends ("value" stocks) will be rising in price faster than anything else. Since economists themselves can never agree on where we are in an economic cycle, it is impossible to know beforehand what new portion of a cycle we will be moving into next.

What are stock-market "cycles" and how do we benefit from them?

The stock market historically has had a 10 percent "correction" about once every 365 days and at least a 20 percent "crash" about once every seven years. These figures are historical averages. Over just the last ten years, we have had two occasions, 2001 and 2008, where the stock market lost first 35 percent and then 50 percent of its value.

In fact, we can now look at the past forty years and note that the market has experienced seven major crashes during that time. In each case, however, there has been a substantial snapback effect that has become reasonably predictable.

As previously mentioned, once we determine the absolute bottom of each crash, the day that marked the lowest point, we can see that the average gain in the following twelve-month period has been 39 percent. The second twelve-month period saw average gains of 12 percent, and the third twelve-month period was 4 percent. With these substantial gains following a downturn, the average long-term annual rise for the years immediately following a crash tended to be 13 percent per year rather than the normally expected 10 percent.

With all these crashes and recoveries, how much can we depend on a 10 percent average return?

We like to think that average returns would be normal over the years and that major crashes and recoveries would happen rarely. Actually, the reverse is true. During the past eighty-four years, stock-market returns were *more than 20 percent per year for about 40 percent of the years.*

The market lost between 0 percent and 10 percent just 14 percent of those years. Significant crashes, like more than 30 percent losses, happened in just 3.6 percent of those eighty-four years.

What we consider to be average returns of somewhere between 0 percent and 20 percent per year happened in just 33 percent of the years. So only about a third of the time can we expect satisfying, "normal" returns that we generally count on. The other two-thirds of the time, we are experiencing losses that make us nervous or gains that make us feel much better about our money management abilities and our futures. It all averages, however, to the 10 percent we like to depend on for future planning.

Dollar-Cost Averaging

Even though this might sound goofy, we *want* to pray that stocks will crash from time to time. When markets decline in value, this is good for voluntary retirement-plan investors. Why? Because we are investing continual infusions of new money every pay period (called dollar-cost averaging). When the stock market falls, this money is buying mutual-fund shares at cheaper and cheaper prices. Each crash and correction allows us to buy shares at bargain prices, which *lowers the average price of all the shares we have purchased.* Years later, when we start nibbling away at our retirement-plan money to generate income for retirement spending, we will be doing what every successful investor pledges to do: buy low and sell high. Today's shares bought at low prices will inevitably be sold years later, bit by bit, at far higher prices. History will repeat itself. And anyone who says, "This time it's different," will be proven wrong.

Rebalancing

Rebalancing is a variation of dollar-cost averaging. If we choose an investment mix today of, say 40 percent bonds and 60 percent stocks, we should rebalance and go back to those proportions once a year if gains on one side have caused the percentage mix to change from our initial balance. This forces us to sell a few shares of the asset type that has increased in value and buy some shares of the cheaper asset. We are methodically selling high and buying low. Rebalancing is explored in greater detail in the next chapter.

While rebalancing offers a mechanical approach to investing, its real value is psychological. There is a huge temptation for amateur investors to try to second-guess what might happen next in the stock market and make investment changes based on a hunch. Fueled by television's financial talking heads and the media in general, investors get very bad advice that prompts them to make disastrous short-term investment decisions.

Rebalancing is simple. It generates time-tested superior results and helps people feel like they take positive steps from one year to the next without having to become market experts.

Besides, who wants to become a market expert when only 15 percent of the professionals actually beat the market averages over long periods? We can't be fooled by those who have beaten the averages recently. They may have been just lucky. There is no way to know who will beat the averages in the future.

The Bottom Line

Dollar-cost averaging and rebalancing are really capitalizing on the extent to which stocks decline in value. On Wall Street, the saying goes, "More money is made in falling markets than in rising markets." This is helpful to remember when markets are crashing and we're still investing or when one of our funds has been struggling and we're prompted by rebalancing to add to that temporary loser.

Once we recognize that the stock market will fluctuate, sometimes wildly, we can capitalize on those fluctuations by understanding how to adopt an investment strategy. Choosing an investment allocation or mix is the subject of the next chapter. This is easier than you might think.

Chapter 8—Choosing Your Investment Mix

By mixing a combination of investment styles, we can reduce our risk and achieve more consistent long-term results. Once we have determined that funds investing in the stock market are appropriate as a part of our retirement-plan investment mix, we need to choose a combination of different investment styles. Why choose different styles? Because diversification is wise—and profitable. With just two mutual funds having the same investment styles, our results would look like this:

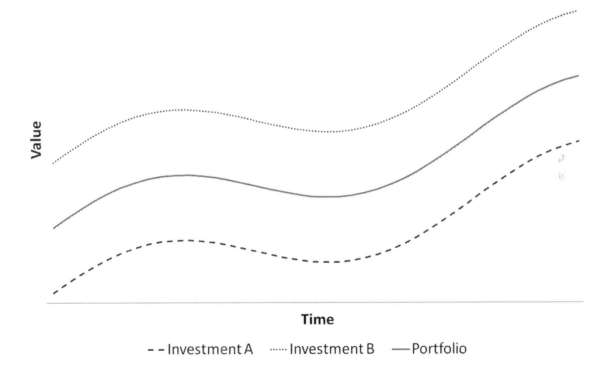

-- Investment A   ······ Investment B   —— Portfolio

With two mutual funds having different styles, our results would look more like this:

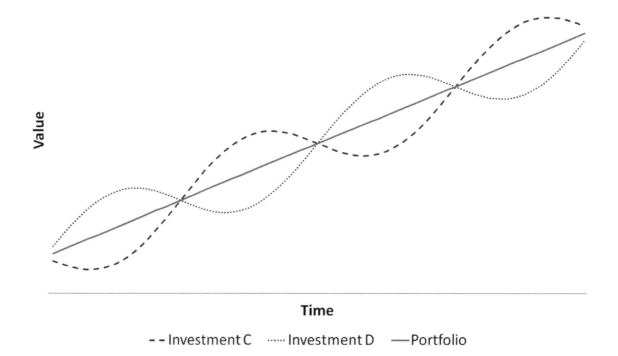

The line up the middle is the "path of minimum regret," a composite result of two investments whose results are said to be "inversely corelated."

Example

In the real world, performance comparisons do not reveal themselves as perfect figure eights like the illustration above. But the following graph representing the actual performance of two mutual-fund types shows how fund performance varies dramatically from year to year. The basic fund types illustrated below are S&P 500 Index and technology.

The chart also illustrates the average return of either both funds combined or the "path of minimum regret." To say the least, it is not a straight line but represents a straighter line than either of the two fund types in the chart.

The Path of Minimum Regret over 20 Years

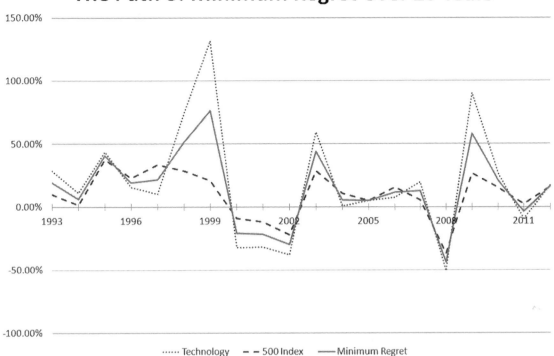

The point: In the world of investing, "Every dog will have its day." It is impossible to predict with any certainty what style will be the next winner. Therefore, you reduce risk by diversifying across a variety of different styles. This concept is called "modern portfolio theory." It is a technique that reduces risk without necessarily reducing returns.

Rebalancing: How to Use the Path of Minimum Regret

As discussed in the previous chapter, rebalancing your investments can help increase returns over long periods. Rebalancing simply means that you sell portions of your winners and buy portions of your losers.

For example, if you started the year with a fifty-fifty mix of a tech fund and an S&P 500 Index fund and assumed a $10,000 annual contribution, your balances at the end of the first year might be $6,000 in the tech fund and $4,000 in the 500 Index fund. In this case, you would sell $1,000 of the tech fund and buy $1,000 of the 500 Index to bring them back to the fifty-fifty allocation.

The following chart shows the growth of an account invested in a two-fund combination. Assuming a $10,000 annual contribution rebalanced each year, the advantage in this example adds up to $40,000 in twenty years. In return for a few minutes of time and some simple arithmetic once a year, the advantage is equal to four full years' worth of contributions.

Fund value with $10,000 annual portfolio contribution (distributed evenly among funds) over twenty-year period:

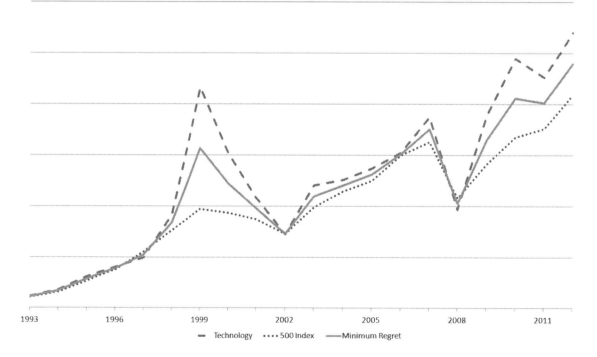

Without Rebalancing

1993   1996   1999   2002   2005   2008   2011

— Technology   ••••500 Index   —Minimum Regret

With Rebalancing

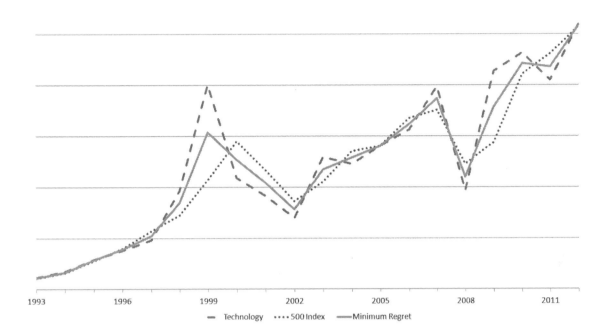

Technology •••• 500 Index Minimum Regret

Market value of Model Portfolio after Twenty Years (1993 to 2012)

Without Rebalancing	With Rebalancing	Rebalancing Advantage
$479,089	$518,225	$39,136

Over time, rebalancing has proven to be probably the best consistently successful investment strategy that investors as a whole have ever developed. We can forget about stock picking (the odds are stacked against us) and/or trying to second-guess where the economy is going next (economists as a group are always famously wrong on that one).

Need more convincing? Let's extend the graph to forty years and assume that the next twenty years will offer the same ups and downs as the past twenty years. Over this hypothetical forty years, the rebalancing mechanism adds, potentially, half a million dollars to the total account balance. When we say "adds," we mean that selling pieces of our winners and adding that money to losers will increase our total nest egg by that much more than we would have had by just setting an allocation and then forgetting it.

Fund Value with $10,000 Annual Portfolio Contribution (Distributed Evenly among Funds) over Forty-Year Period

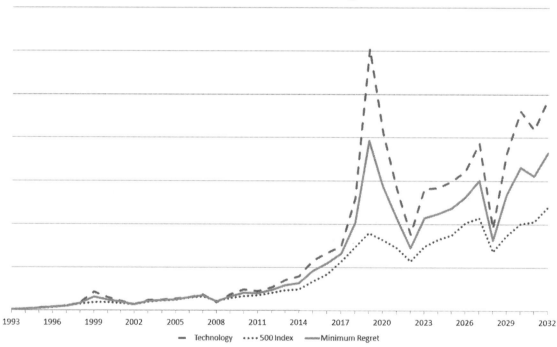

Without Rebalancing

With Rebalancing

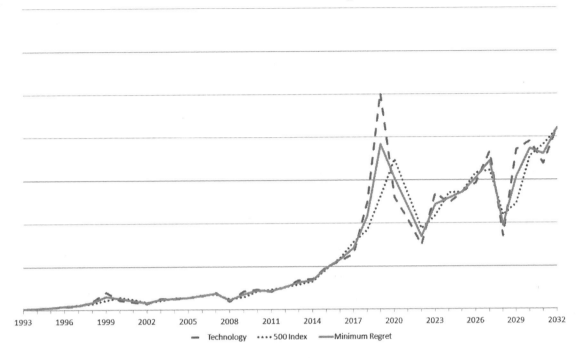

Technology ····· 500 Index ——Minimum Regret

Market Value of Model Portfolio after Forty Years (1993 to 2032)

Without Rebalancing	With Rebalancing	Rebalancing Advantage
$3,653,246	$4,211,530	$558284

What is the biggest risk facing an investor?

The biggest investment risk for a retirement-plan investor is the risk of abandoning a strategy. Once an investor has determined the time required for their retirement-plan goals and has chosen an investment mix for those goals, the most important factor generating future success is not deviating from that strategy. In other words, we should hold steady.

People who freaked out in 1987, 2000, or 2008 and moved into money-market funds missed out on the opportunity to be even again within, at most, two years. Those who moved to cash typically lost 20 percent and did not return to the market until it was once again poised for the next crash. (Talk about snapping defeat from the jaws of victory!)

A mechanical approach to the market, coupled with confidence in history's ability to repeat itself, can make anyone a winner in managing their financial future.

When it comes to rebalancing, the positive arithmetic is probably not as important as the psychological value of this exercise. Understanding that successful investors tend to buy losers (when they are relatively cheap) and sell winners (when they become relatively expensive) is an important methodology to incorporate into your investment practices. The all-too-popular but disastrous alternative is to chase last year's best-performing fund. Yet studies show that this practice is what most amateur investors do year after year.

Worse yet is the practice of bailing out of the market after watching assets drop by 15 to 20 percent. Moving into cash or money-market funds at that point dooms the now-traumatized investor to missing out on the inevitable snapback. Anyone fleeing the market will be waiting until they are absolutely certain of the market's health before tiptoeing back in. Meanwhile, remember that 39 percent average first-year return from the bottom of a crash? Roughly 20 percent of the average 39 percent occurs *during the first four to six weeks*. The train is leaving the station and everyone wants to get on—right now.

The primary benefit to a disciplined rebalancing strategy is that it prevents us from making the classic mistake of buying high and selling low.

Adding Bond Funds to the Rebalancing Exercise Further Reduces Risk

So far, we have been rebalancing just different types of stock-invested mutual funds. If we add bond funds to the mix, we can further reduce our risk, and in wildly fluctuating markets like those of the past ten years, we can actually increase our returns.

An all-stock mix can be expected to gain roughly 10 percent per year over long periods, but two-thirds of the years we are invested in that mix the results will range between a 27 percent gain and a 7 percent loss. (This is referred to as one "standard deviation.")

If we change the mix to have one-third of the money invested in bond mutual funds and the other two-thirds in stocks, then the expected return for two-thirds of the years we are invested ranges between a gain of 22 percent and a loss of just 2 percent. Instead of an average gain of 10 percent that an all-stock mix would have been providing, we would need to be satisfied with just 9 percent. We give up 1 percent of possible annual gain for the safety of a lower loss.

One-third bonds and two-thirds stocks has proven to be the "sweet spot" of any mix between stocks and bonds. As you move to a greater percentage of bonds, the potential gain drops to 7.5 percent (at a fifty-fifty mix), and the downside protection is not much greater.

Rebalancing a mix between stock funds and bond funds, however, can be more rewarding in some years than just rebalancing an all-stock mix of different styles. Why? Because stock and bond prices often move in opposite directions (they are said to be inversely correlated), and the effect of rebalancing can be more dramatic.

We're Approaching the Finish Line ...

The exercise of rebalancing annually and eventually folding in some bond funds as retirement looms is a basic investment pattern for a lifetime of investing. The last chapter illustrates how we need to manage our money in retirement, but the last few years of our career give us the opportunity for a dry run. Gaining some experience and a comfort level with a mix of stock and bond funds is better accomplished while we're still working. Adding some bond funds to the mix should start about ten years before that final day at work.

Chapter 9—Managing "Other Money"

While most of our money is invested in 401(k)s, 403(b)s, IRAs, and other retirement plans, some Americans are fortunate enough to have so-called "after-tax money." This is money that is not in tax-free retirement plans. It's just a prudent result of having managed to save and invest some "take-home" pay. After-tax money can also come from other sources, such as inheritances, the sale of a home or business, stock options, divorce settlements, and financial events that don't involve retirement plans.

These after-tax dollars can be much more difficult to accumulate for two reasons. First, if you started with $1,000 of gross investment earnings, you would have to pay taxes and then save what is left. For many people, state and federal income taxes on their last $1,000 of earnings can easily be as much as 35 percent combined. That would leave about $650 after taxes to be invested. It gets worse, because then you're taxed each year on your success as an investor. For these reasons, after-tax money is a challenge to grow. As a result, special investment techniques and different types of mutual funds can be brought into play to meet this greater challenge.

Before going farther, let's review one of the basics. The "Rule of 72" describes the fact that money earning 10 percent per year doubles every 7.2 years. Therefore, $1,000 today will be $2,000 in 7.2 years, $4,000 in 14.4 years, $8,000 in 21.6 years, etc. Money earning 7.2 percent by comparison doubles every ten years, so at this rate, $1,000 will be $2,000 in ten years and $4,000 in twenty years. That's the magic of compound interest. The first year's $1,000 earning 10 percent becomes next year's $1,100 earning another 10 percent or $110, etc.

Unless an investor is retired, these investment earnings will be accumulating on top of what is already their earned income from a job. So now, let's review a second basic.

Generally speaking, you don't pay much in taxes on the first half of your income. Instead, the government chooses to really "sock it to you" on the last half of what you make. It is taxing at an ever-increasing percentage as your income increases.

Remember the last time you received what was supposed to be a $100 raise per paycheck? You probably noticed that your new take-home pay increased by only about $65. The reason the increase was small compared to your gross wage increase was because that raise was the last $100 of your income and was taxed at the highest rate you pay.

The following schedule will help you calculate the tax rate on each additional amount of money you receive in income. These tax percentages are known as your marginal tax rates because they illustrate the rate that you pay at the outer limit of your income.

Approximate "Marginal" Income Tax Percentages
(percent tax on the last $1,000 of income)

Includes Both Federal and Approximate California State Taxes

Single Persons		Married Persons *	
Taxable Income	**% Tax**	**Taxable Income**	**% Tax**
$8,925 to $36,250	18%	$17,850 to $72,500	20%
$36,250 to $87,850	33%	$72,500 to $146,400	33%
$87,850 to $183,250	37%	$146,400 to $223,050	37%

* If your spouse is also working, use your combined income to estimate your marginal income tax brackets.

** Remember that for each exemption you claim, subtract $3,900 from your taxable income.

When income from after-tax investments is reported each year, it gets added to the taxable income of a single person or a couple filing jointly. Unless you plan to quit working, your investment income becomes the "extra" income (just like getting a raise in the example above) that gets taxed at the highest marginal rate. Therefore, a 10 percent return on an after-tax investment might net only about 6.5 percent after taxes. By comparison, the same 10 percent earned in a retirement plan would still be a full 10 percent added to the growing tax-deferred account balance.

Here's an example. Sally and Jim both work and have a taxable income after all deductions and exemptions of $69,000. Sally inherits $200,000 from a relative and they deposit this into a bond mutual fund that pays interest at a rate of 5 percent, which amounts to $10,000 per year. This $10,000, even if they don't spend it, raises the couple's taxable income to $79,000 for the year. We can see from the chart above that all dollars between $68,789 and $86,934 are taxed at 33 percent. This means that Sally and Jim will owe an additional $3,300 in taxes on the $10,000, leaving them with just $6,700 to add to the $200,000 account.

Now you can see why investing after-tax money can be such a challenge. Not all fund earnings, fortunately, are taxed as regular income like the previous example. So-called "capital gains" income is taxed at a combined rate (California state and federal) of 25 percent. This is income that comes not from regular interest paid but from the profitable sale of an Investment—selling your stock, for instance, at a price higher than the initial purchase.

How Mutual-Fund Profits Are Taxed

When mutual funds investing in stocks throughout the year buy and sell different companies, they generate profitable trades (hopefully) that add up to gains that are taxable for the year. At the end of each year, investors in those mutual funds receive a form 1099 detailing their share of those taxable gains. This information goes on our tax return, and we pay taxes on those amounts accordingly. Then, when we sell a mutual fund years later at a higher price than we paid for it, we calculate the difference in price (for example, we bought it for $1,000 and we're selling it seven years later for $2,000) and we owe taxes on that profit. However, we are allowed to reduce our profit by all the gains that we paid taxes on over the seven years that we owned the fund. It's complicated, of course, which explains why most people have much better investment results in their tax-insensitive retirement accounts.

What investment types are most tax friendly?

So how do we manage to minimize the tax hit on our after-tax money? Index funds, tax-managed mutual funds, and annuities offer some of the best tax shelters outside of a retirement plan.

Index Funds

Index funds just invest in a broad cross-section of companies within a specific type. For example, the S&P 500 Index invests in the largest five hundred companies in the country. The Vanguard Small Cap Index Fund invests only in a cross-section of small companies. Index funds are "passively" managed, which means that no one is actively trying to find the next super-star company. As a result, these funds have very little turnover of buying and selling. A typical amount might be as little as 5 percent of the total portfolio per year. By comparison, some mutual funds have 200 percent turnover, which means they have replaced by June all the companies they owned in January, and by December, they have sold once again the new companies they had owned in June.

An index fund that does very little trading generates very little in ongoing annual capital gains profits that would otherwise trigger annual taxable income. Years later, when a portion of the fund is sold at a profit, there is little in the way of annual gains that have been reported along the way. What would have been paid in taxes is still sitting in the investment and is part of what becomes the gain that the investor gets to enjoy. The distinction offered by index funds is that the profits are controlled by the investor rather than by the fund company. Taxes are due only on the profit made on the amount of money withdrawn from the fund in a year. Someone nibbling away at their index funds to support themselves in retirement might be paying relatively little in taxes on the distributions from their index funds.

Tax-Managed Mutual Funds and Other Tax-Reduction Products

Tax-managed mutual funds are those that are sensitive to the tax hit, so they solve this problem by selling some stocks at a profit each year while "harvesting losses" that will offset the gains. The net effect is that their investors reviewing their year-end 1099 tax reports from the fund will see that they will not have to come up with more money for taxes.

Some bond funds invest in so-called "tax free munis," which are municipal bonds that offer interest that is free of federal and state income taxes. Usually, these bonds pay an interest rate that is lower than that of taxable bonds because they recognize that their tax-free treatment gives them an advantage that allows them to pay less interest.

Annuities are insurance products that allow investors to accumulate money in tax-deferred shelters, just like that of retirement plans. However, annuities can be very expensive and come loaded with all forms of commissions, death benefits, and something called "contingent deferred sales charges," which are penalties for withdrawing your money.

ETFs are exchange-traded funds, like index mutual funds, but they are valued minute by minute and traded throughout the day. Traditional mutual funds are valued just once at the end of each day. The advantage is that an investor can control when the stocks in the fund are sold. ETFs are relatively new financial products that are sold through the brokerage industry. You pay an annual expense, as you would with any mutual fund, but you also pay a brokerage or transaction fee to buy the ETF.

Investment Real Estate

Owning investment real estate offers a tax shelter because depreciation, mortgage interest, and other expenses are tax deductible. These deductible expenses offset what would have been taxable profits from just collecting rent and paying expenses. Investment real estate involves a tremendous degree of risk and a lot of work if investing requires hands-on managing of the property yourself. Most people who consider buying single-family homes in the aftermath of the housing collapse might be wise to go lie on a beach until that thought goes away. Unlike apartment buildings, which can generate positive cash flow from month to month, most single-family homes make money for the investor only if the rising value is high enough to offset the negative cash flow.

Part-Time Business

Operating a part-time business can offer an investment opportunity for after-tax dollars. In return for the after-tax investment, the business itself becomes a tax shelter. Here is an example. One of my friends makes fish sculptures out of driftwood and sells them for a total gross income of about $10,000 per year. As a result, he is allowed a write-off, a deduction from income for the cost of owning his boat. In addition, a business that is profitable can allow its owners a tax-deductible contribution of the first $17,000 of income directly into a 401(k) plan. This is a so-called "solo 401(k)" designed for small businesses. Small businesses offer a multitude of opportunities to characterize what would be normal activities of daily life as legitimate business expenses.

The Mental Challenge of After-Tax Money

Investing after-tax money can be complicated. Before taking some profits and investing in another opportunity, we need to ask, "Will making this change compensate for the tax cost that the sale will trigger?" The expense of paying the tax will be a loss with 100 percent certainty. In many cases, staying the course will be a better option.

Further complicating after-tax investing are the discoveries being made in the field of behavioral finance. This is the area of psychology that studies how people make investment decisions, and the results are discouraging. We are our own worst enemies. In simple terms, the greater the number of choices, the less inclined we are to make a decision. It's known as "the status quo bias" or, more commonly, "analysis paralysis." Sometimes, however, it's not so bad if it prevents us from making what would have been a bad investment on an impulse.

Fear of loss is a more powerful emotion than the exhilaration we experience from enjoying investment success. We are far more disappointed if we lose money after making an investment change than would have been the case if we hadn't done anything and lost money as a result. These psychological factors conspire to make it a challenge to manage money. However, psychological factors come into play to a greater degree with after-tax money because the choices are so vast and the decisions are more complex.

The bottom line with after-tax money is to try to make it comparable (as much as possible) to your retirement-plan money. Invest in index funds and other investment products outlined above that offer at least some tax shelter. Then rebalance systematically. Rebalancing introduces a mechanical aspect to investing that takes the emotion out of decision-making. The perils of behavioral finance fall by the wayside. Go for runs batted in (RBIs) rather than home runs. The tax hits, when they come, will be incremental and relatively slight from year to year. Those who are content with making money slowly are guaranteed to succeed over time.

Chapter 10—The End Game

Living a life without exhausting your retirement resources

Part 2 of this book outlines the basic fundamentals you will need to know and practice to get the most out of your retirement nest egg.

To summarize and set the hook for what you'll learn in the upcoming section, there are three important fundamentals:

1. Social security will pay somewhere between $25,000 and $50,000 per year graded up by cost of living increases. It won't go broke any more than our military will go broke. There is a $2.3 trillion dollar surplus right now, which was created in anticipation of retiring baby boomers.

2. Your 401(k) and other retirement money divided equally between bond and stock mutual funds will provide an annual income equal to 5 percent of your total nest egg. Hopefully, this 5 percent figure (about $12,000 per year on a $240,000 balance or $25,000 per year on a $500,000 balance) will be enough—when combined with social security to meet your retirement income needs.

3. Working the system involves rolling all of your retirement money into an individual retirement account (IRA) so that you have complete control of the money without having had to pay any taxes or penalties. Having the money all in one place makes it easier to invest purposefully. Moreover, you can direct the financial institution housing your mutual funds to automatically deposit each month's income (dividends and interest) directly into your checking account.

Why is the end game important to think about now?

Understanding the end game helps to zero in on what needs to be accomplished between now and retirement. After social security, each thousand dollars a month of retirement income will require about $250,000 in retirement assets. A million dollars safely generates about $4,000 a month of income.

While these numbers may seem overwhelming, you may be in better shape than you think. The real magic of compound interest starts to take place toward the end of our retirement investing experience. Take, for instance, the money you have in retirement accounts today and double the amount every seven years into the future until you reach age sixty-six or thereabouts. For instance, if you have $50,000 in retirement accounts today and you're age fifty, that $50,000 should double twice to $200,000 by the time you reach age sixty-five. *Remember that money earning 10 percent per year doubles every 7.2 years.*

Then you have new inbound contributions. If you're fifty years old today, a $500 per month contribution for fifteen years will grow to $250,000 by age sixty-five at a 10 percent earnings rate. $1,000 per month will grow to $500,000. A total of $2,000 per month as a result of, say, two spouses each contributing to their retirement plans should grow to $1,000,000 in just fifteen years.

Add this "new money" formed by future contributions to your "old money" that doubles every seven years. The sum of the parts should be a pleasant surprise

What It's All About …

In a perfect world, we want to have the resources to enjoy our lives in nice surroundings with independence and care when we need it. Getting to that stage with enough money is the ultimate goal of retirement planning. Planning the work is one thing. Working the plan comes from applying the tools in this booklet and gaining the satisfaction that comes with self-discipline. This "roadmap to riches" shows you how to get there. Go ahead. Fasten your seatbelt, turn on the ignition, and step on the gas.

Part 2—How to Live a Life and Not Outlive Your Retirement Resources

Chapter 11—Introduction

Today, seventy-five thousand Americans are older than one hundred—and one third of them are still driving. That could be you, someday. The purpose of this section of the book is to help you retain the financial resources to make anything within reason a possibility throughout your retirement years.

The 401(k) investor who has sacrificed to accumulate money over the years eventually reaches a retirement date and begins living that eccentric personal lifestyle—the fantasy of what life would be like with no commute, no cubicle, and no work-related stress.

All the years of retirement-plan participation have been enhanced by employer contributions, videos and seminars from financial institutions, discussions with fellow employees, and all the general hoopla surrounding the 401(k) and/or 403(b) phenomenon. But newly minted retirees, the day they walk out the door, are alone with their money.

Any professional offering to help introduces at least some conflict of interest, so the more we can learn about the basics of retirement planning and investing, the more judiciously we can manage the professionals and organizations who profess to be there to help us. Anyone who has heard the name Madoff will understand the extent to which depending on others, out of ignorance, can lead to disappointing results—if not disaster. There's no substitute for ongoing education and a healthy level of skepticism.

Throughout the accumulation stage, retirement-plan participants have been focused on accumulating assets. Apart from enduring market downdrafts, nothing really emotionally challenging accompanies this stage, beyond just self-discipline. There's always more time to keep saving, and on the whole, markets and mutual funds rise in value sooner or later.

Shifting gears to fund a retirement lifestyle is entirely different. There's the sense that "This is it." The idea that retirement money has to last a lifetime is bothersome if not scary. If you're close to retirement yourself, you'll notice that your retired friends seem to be obsessed with not overspending—getting deals whenever possible—regardless of how substantial they may be financially. All that emotional energy once focused on a professional or entrepreneurial experience is now focused on spending money wisely.

There's no need to panic. We will start by describing the end result of what retirement income will look like and where the money will come from. Then we'll peel away the layers of the onion to help you understand the fundamentals that will build confidence and contribute to your success. The result will be a step-by-step guide to meeting retirement objectives.

The chance that we might outlive our financial resources over the years of retirement is always lurking. For what could easily be more than thirty years of retirement living, inflation itself is the silent killer of retirement asset values over long periods of time. The ideas we have explored here should offer a helpful rundown of the basics, and a portion of our strategy is designed to combat the ravages of inflation.

The key to success is to keep the plan simple and avoid mistakes. Retirees suffer disappointing results when they chase the previous year's best performing funds or succumb to something that sounds too good to be true. If it's any consolation, some of the smartest financial minds got taken in by Bernie Madoff's "12 percent return per year—rain or shine." How smart? Try the former CEO of one of the nation's largest brokerage firms.

We all make mistakes, starting with Merrill Lynch when it went bankrupt and had to be rescued by (effectively) us taxpayers. Every one of us has a "woulda, shoulda, coulda" story. The purpose of this book is to lay out some of the basics and set the stage for the successful financial management during this final chapter of our investment experience.

Chapter 12—Show Me the Money

How will we pay our bills?

Finally … After All These Years

Social security will be the bedrock of everyone's retirement plan. The dollar amount will be substantial and virtually guaranteed by the US government. You can set aside all the scare stories about the program running out of money. What will happen, eventually, is that the annual social security tax will go up while the age at which retirees begin receiving income will be progressively adjusted to older ages. As part of this effort, financial incentives to postpone benefits will be increased. The system will not go broke and leave us with nothing. After all, we currently have a reserve of $2.5 trillion today because, thanks to Ronald Reagan who doubled the social security tax during his presidency, we anticipated this "bubble" of demand.

For people who have worked all of their adult lives, social security benefits can be surprisingly generous. Where over 60 percent of all married couples have two family incomes, both family members receive benefits in their retirement years, and the total for today's retired couples can be over $30,000 per year. A single fifty-six-year-old employee earning $60,000 today who has worked for thirty years thus far is scheduled to receive $29,500 per year if they retire in ten years. A forty-six-year-old, earning $60,000 today, who has worked for twenty years so far can expect to receive $32,500 per year if they retire in twenty years. If married, their spouse who receives 50 percent as a dependent benefit will get $16,250, which brings the total social security income to an annual $48,750 per year. Moreover, these benefits rise with a cost-of-living percentage increase once retirement begins.

Life beyond Social Security

So much for social security, but where will we find other income to meet the rest of our retirement living expenses? Other resources include retirement accounts like 401(k)'s, IRAs, and other retirement plans. Then for most people, there will be some combination of home equity, inheritances, regular nonretirement savings and investments, a pension plan resulting from government or large-company employment, the sale of a business or stock options, and finally, we shouldn't rule out part-time work—if only to maintain sanity.

Investment accounts designed to generate income for retirement typically use a combination of stock and bond mutual funds. Bonds, of course, are loans to corporations or governments that pay interest. Stocks represent ownership in companies and pay dividends while rising in value at typically better than the rate of inflation.

Half Bonds/Half Stocks—Keeping It Simple

An ideal mix for a newly retired person is a fifty-fifty combination of stock and bond mutual funds. The stock mutual funds (investing in large value-oriented companies) will typically pay dividends equal to about 4 percent. A combination of bond mutual funds (described in a later chapter) will pay average interest rates of about 6 percent per year. You can do the math. If half of your money is earning 4 percent per year in stock mutual-fund dividends, that would amount to 2 percent of your total investment. If the other half is earning 6 percent in bond mutual-fund interest, that would be 3 percent of your total investment. The combined annual return, paid in cash, for the two halves added together would be 5 percent.

So if you are someone with $240,000 in a combination of IRAs, 401(k), and other retirement plans, you would be earning an annual 5 percent or $12,000 per year in interest and dividends without touching any portion of your principal (otherwise known as your "nest egg.") The basic $240,000 nest egg remains untouched, and all you are spending is the $1,000 per month of the $12,000 annual income. What you are really preserving—critical in the early retirement years—is your golden goose.

Let's Be Practical

Working the system involves rolling all of your retirement money into an individual retirement account (IRA) so that you have complete control of the money without having pay any taxes or penalties. Having the money all in one place makes it easier to invest purposefully. Moreover, you can direct the financial institution housing your mutual funds to automatically deposit each month's income (dividends and interest) directly into your checking account. Money just automatically flows into the account to supplement social security deposits that the government will be wiring into your account.

When to Tap the Nest Egg

If you need additional money, you can always pick up the phone and ask the financial institution to wire an additional lump sum into your account. This amounts to plucking a few tail feathers off of the goose—not that there's anything wrong with that. A new car, a new roof, or a vacation trip while everyone's still healthy can be valid reasons for invading the principal.

In many cases, the stock mutual-fund portion of the principal may have increased substantially in favorable markets. Remember stocks in general tend to increase in value by about 10 percent per year. Not every year, certainly, but over time, we can expect this to happen. Taking a few chips off the table after a string of good years is nothing to be shy about.

The greatest mistake a retiree can make is to spend too much of his or her retirement money in the early years of retirement. Spending money at the time the market itself might also be plummeting amounts to a perfect storm of financial devastation. This is why many so-called "glide path" programs that are set to have you run out of money at age ninety have proven to be such a disaster in the few short years since they have been "invented." The same would be true of financial advisors that tell retiree clients what the latter want to hear—namely, that future investment results will more than compensate for any invasion of the nest egg.

What we have just provided is an overview of what a retirement financial picture will look like. Relax. The following chapters will fill in the details and explain the fundamentals in a way that is designed to build confidence in both your abilities and the system itself.

Chapter 13—Where to Take Your Money

What institutions can we trust?

What to Avoid

Once you have crossed the Rubicon into retirement—a world in which you have no more earned income and are depending on your investments to supplement social security—the choice of investment institutions is critical. Assuming you're determined to gain some education and follow the lessons in this book, step 1 is to avoid the retail brokerage industry. Step 2 is to avoid banks. This leaves just the no-load mutual-fund industry. The term *no-load* means that there are no commissioned sales people selling the funds—commissions you want to avoid paying at all costs. The two confidence-inspiring giants in the world of no-load fund families are Fidelity and Vanguard, but other no-load fund companies include Dodge and Cox and T. Rowe Price.

It is critical to generate at least a 5 percent income return from the assets in your retirement for reasons we spelled out in the opening chapter. If you are paying one full percentage point to have money managed or investments sold to you, it will reduce your net income to 4 percent—a 20 percent reduction in spending money. Brokerage firms have to make this 1 percent (and actually far more) to stay in business. Many financial planners charge 1 percent per year. Banks pay next to nothing on CDs today, so they are under pressure to sell highly profitable annuities. The income from annuities may sound good until you realize that they are systematically spending your principal to provide the income.

For the average retiree, mutual-fund companies offer by far the best investment "platform." Investing in individual stocks is a sucker's game. The average small investor loses money over any five-year period when working with a major national brokerage firm. It's the sad truth behind the old question, "Where are the customers' yachts?" We read today that Goldman Sachs made billions recently by betting on the fall in value (selling "short") of the investments they were recommending to their customers. At the same time, Merrill Lynch (the "thundering herd") was leveraged over thirty to one and its insolvency drove it into the arms of Bank of America—both of which were then kept alive only by an infusion of taxpayer money. We can forget the full-service brokerage and banking industries.

A so-called "discount" brokerage firm like Charles Schwab or TD Ameritrade can offer funds in its mutual-fund marketplace, and the idea is that all your money is located at one place regardless of any combination of mutual funds you have. This is further enhanced by the possibility of there being no transaction fees if you move money from one fund to another—or have monthly distributions made to your checking account. There is a major problem with this approach. For funds to be offered in the "no-transaction fee" (NTF) program, those funds electing this successful marketing channel have to pay the discount houses almost 0.5 percent per year. Funds in an NTF program charge the investor an annual expense ratio (a percent of assets) high enough to cover what is basically a marketing expense. Basically, investors are being charged for the "no-transaction-fee" option, but the charge is buried in higher annual expense ratios.

A very cost-effective ("cheap") fund might charge as little as 0.12 percent per year as a percent of assets. On $100,000, this would amount to $120. It is a cost for which no investor ever receives a bill or has to write a check. The mutual-fund industry is set up to just automatically deduct the money from earnings on a daily basis throughout the year as it "harvests" its total of $120. Meanwhile, in a fund that qualifies to be on a no-transaction-fee fund list, the average annual expense ratio would typically be in the 1.5 percentage point range. This means that on the same $100,000, the annual cost is $1,500 (and rising as the asset amount increases.) These mutual-fund marketplaces tend to offer better deals to investors who will pay a one-time transaction fee to move money into a high-quality low-cost fund.

The other alternative is to go directly to your favorite fund family, or families, and avoid any transaction fees. Vanguard, for example, refuses to pay anything to anybody, so the only way to avoid transaction fees when using its funds is to go to Vanguard directly.

Vanguard is unique as a financial service firm because it is operated like a giant cooperative. There are no owners other than the mutual fund-investors who invest with them. Therefore, the best place for IRA money is the Vanguard family of funds. Not only can you access hundreds of its low-cost investment products with no transaction fees, but you can also purchase, at Vanguard, any stocks, bonds or other mutual funds sold in this country. This is made possible because within Vanguard itself, there is a brokerage services division, which is effectively a discount brokerage firm. Whatever your investments at Vanguard might be, they all show up on the same statement.

To its credit, Fidelity also offers a similar level of flexibility and spectrum of investment choice. The only drawback is that its fund selection does not offer as many index funds and its so-called "core" funds charge more than those at Vanguard. Ironically, you can invest in Vanguard funds through Fidelity at its brokerage services site, but you will be charged a transaction fee.

The website for downloading forms and information is www.vanguard.com.

The website for Fidelity is www.fidelity.com.

As soon as possible, develop a relationship with one of these companies to gain confidence and a comfort level with long-distance financial services and management. We know there's a temptation to lean toward regional institutions with "bricks and mortar" that can be visited in person. The cost of that preference, however, might cost as much as $10,000 a year in substandard investment choices and high fees.

Chapter 14—A Case Study of Retirement Finance

A Real-Life Look at Retirement Income Sources

Joe Smith worked for forty-five years, and at the end of his career, he was earning $60,000. His wife, Linda, had worked early in their marriage and then stopped working to raise their children. When the kids were finally out of the house, she rejoined the work force and accumulated additional social security credits. Between the two spouses, social security benefits totaled $35,000 per year or almost $3,000 per month by the time both retired at age sixty-six.

Combined 401(k) and other retirement-plan assets totaled $500,000. Over the years, they had saved about 6 percent of their annual income on average—the last thirty years in 401(k) contributions. A higher balance would have been nice, but college education expenses had stood in the way of more effective retirement investing. By the time college costs had been covered, it was too late for the "magic of compound interest" to be of much help with such a short time left until retirement.

However, with both spouses working, substantial 401(k) contributions (maximum $23,000 by each) had helped create a last-minute boost of account balances. Because there was no percentage-of-income limitation, Linda was able to deposit over half of her $40,000 salary into her company's 401(k). (If she had made only $23,000 working part-time, the entire amount could have been contributed into a 401(k).) Fortunately, their house was now paid for, so a major living expense was no longer a factor. With a combined income of $100,000, Joe and Linda's combined $46,000 contribution cost only $30,000 in take-home pay. This is because about $14,000 consisted of money that Joe and Linda would otherwise have owed in additional taxes on their last $46,000 of family income without the 401(k) tax shelter.

Below is what retirement looked like for the Smiths. Their investment mix included the following funds:

Stock Fund—50 percent

- Vanguard Value Index. Average dividend paid over the years was approximately 4 percent.

Bond Funds—50 percent split equally

- Vanguard Short-Term Investment Grade. Average interest in recent years was 4.5 percent.
- Vanguard GNMA Fund. Average interest in recent years was 5.5 percent.
- Vanguard High Yield Corporate Bond. Average interest in recent years was 7.5 percent.

Average for three bond funds, in round numbers, is 6 percent per year.

$250,000 in a stock fund yielded about $10,000 per year.

$250,000 in bond funds yielded $15,000 per year.

This $25,000, deposited automatically into the Smiths' checking account, combined with the $35,000 from social security, creates a total income of $60,000. This is the same $60,000 that Joe had earned in his last years of work. But wait. There are no social security or Medicare taxes charged to retirement income. This saves Joe and Linda about $6,000 that they used to pay on Joe's $60,000 of job income.

Bottom Line ...

In take-home pay, this couple is very close to where they were before Linda went back to work. A possible rise in value of the stock portion of their retirement plan and the cost-of-living increases in social security help to protect them from inflation. Moreover, they may decide to downsize after rattling around in a house that once sheltered a family of four plus pets, but that decision can come much later in retirement. In the meantime, the house offers yet another buffer against inflation.

Protecting against inflation is critical for the retiree, because the cost of health care will continue to rise faster than Medicare and social security can keep up. In a perfect world, we all want to have the resources to live out our lives in nice surroundings with plenty of care. Getting to that stage with enough resources is the ultimate goal of retirement planning.

Chapter 15—More on Bonds—How They Work

How can we earn more interest and be comfortable with the risk?

Because an understanding of bonds is so crucial to generating income for retirees, some of what was mentioned about them in part 1 of the book bears repeating here (especially for those who might have skipped part 1.)

Stocks are relatively easy to understand, but bonds can be confusing. For retirees, bonds and bond mutual funds are key investment products that become the cornerstones of safety and secure incomes. What's confusing to investors is that bond prices can rise and fall even if the interest payments remain constant. All too often, people who don't understand the reasons for these temporary changes in value simply retreat into money-market funds, annuities, CDs, and other guaranteed investment products that typically pay less in interest. A basic understanding of bonds and bond funds can help a retiree capture what otherwise would have been bank or insurance-company profits—and increase that retiree's interest income by as much as 50 percent.

How Bonds Work

To illustrate how bonds work, we will buy a five-year bond that sells for $1,000 and that pays (to keep the arithmetic simple) a 10 percent interest rate. This means that the bond is effectively a loan that will pay the investor $100 per year and return the original $1,000 at the end of five years.

The 10 percent rate of return when the bond was brand new was what the going market rate for five-year loans happened to be at the time we purchased the bond. Over the five-year holding period, however, the market rate for new bonds sold to other people fluctuated between 8 percent and 12 percent because of different events taking place in the economy that affected interest rates in general.

Because bonds are priced every day, just like stocks, the price of a previously issued bond can go down if interest rates in the market go up. Why? Because our old bond (in this example) paying just $100 per year has to compete with a brand-new bond that someone can buy that will pay them $120 per year. If we were desperate to sell our bond, we would have to reduce the price to about

$800 so that our $100 annual interest payment, (the coupon) would equal a 12 percent return on the $800 purchase price.

On the other hand, if interest rates in the market had dropped to 8 percent, a brand-new bond would only be paying $80 per year. We have a valuable old bond that pays $100, so we could actually sell our bond for about $1,200 to another bond buyer (our $100 annual interest equals about an 8 percent return on $1,200) and effectively make a $200 profit.

As our bond approaches its maturity—the point at which we get the $1,000 back—the fluctuation in price goes away regardless of what is happening in the interest rate market. This is because we are close enough to the end point and nobody is interested in buying our bond for such a short holding period.

A Simple Example

In general, bond prices change in ways that resemble a rope draped over a pulley. If one side of the rope drops (falling interest rates in the economy), the other side of the rope goes up (capital value of our bond.) If interest rates rise, capital value goes down. When the bond reaches maturity, we're effectively buying a new rope and pulley after getting all our money back from the first.

One popular technique for buying bonds is called "laddering." Basically, it calls for building a bond "ladder" with bonds that have different maturity dates so that at least some bonds will always be close to maturity and close to coming due. These are the bonds that will be rolled over into new bonds at whatever the new interest rate happens to be.

Bond Mutual Funds

An investment in a bond mutual fund is different from an investment in a single bond or a group of individual bonds. With individual bonds, we have control over the maturity date. If we think interest rates are going to go up, and we're concerned about a temporary drop in capital value, we can limit ourselves to buying short-term bonds, or we can hold our long-term bonds until they reach or approach maturity.

With a bond mutual fund, we own a proportionate share of a huge, multibillion-dollar collection of bonds together with thousands of other investors. In this mutual-fund pool, there are some bonds reaching maturity and being rolled over into new ones every business day. Some bond mutual funds have all of their bonds reaching maturity in relatively short time periods—like within two years. These bond funds have very little capital value fluctuation because too many of their bonds are reaching maturity and are being replaced with brand-new bonds at whatever the new interest rate happens to be. There's not enough time for capital value fluctuations. On the other hand, there can be bond funds that have longer average maturities, such as seven to ten years. These bond funds can have a lot of changes in their capital values, but over time, they always revert to the norm—meaning that they return to their original value.

For the bond fund investor, the trick is to learn to ignore these changes in capital value. Assume that you will own the bond fund to perpetuity. Sooner or later, all of the bonds reach maturity and any capital value fluctuations iron themselves out. Anyone turning to bond funds to generate a long-term income stream in retirement can "set it and forget it."

Three Choices, Each with a Different Purpose

There is a specific purpose for each of the bond funds recommended in the previous chapter.

1. The short-term corporate bond fund is designed to be one step up from a money-market fund. It can have some capital value fluctuation, but not much. This is the fund that someone would tap for a major expense or an investment elsewhere.
2. The GNMA fund involves longer time periods to maturity for its bonds, but these bonds are invested in government-guaranteed mortgages. GNMA fund will typically pay the rate of interest that we read about as the average mortgage interest rate. The capital is guaranteed by the US government, so there is no default risk—default meaning the fact that the borrower goes bankrupt and can't pay.
3. The high-yield corporate fund which is investing in bonds that are below (just below) so-called "investment grade." Investment grade bonds are those that are loans to corporations so solid that they could never be expected to default. By comparison, "high-yield" refers to bonds purchased from companies that could, in fact, be expected to default under some rare circumstances. However, even these high-yield bonds rarely default and the interest rates paid because they might default are substantial enough to offset any expected defaults. This explains why a high-yield bond fund tends to generate income in the 7 to 8 percent range in recent years. It is a premium rate of return, and this extra 2 to 3 percent is referred to in finance as the "risk premium." High-yield bond funds perform more like stock funds with respect to fluctuations in their capital values. They lost about 30 percent during the most recent crash but made all the money back in 2009. These funds tend to revert to the norm, sooner or later, but a retiree should expect to keep them for an entire retirement lifetime so that the value fluctuations can be ignored.

Higher Risk but Worthwhile Reward

While most bond funds do regain their values sooner or later, there is an advisory heads-up regarding high-yield corporate bond funds. While some of the more conservative high-yield bond funds have rarely had a default, they have sometimes sold bonds at a loss because their judgment suggested that the bonds might default before they reached maturity. As a result, the long-term capital value of high-yield bond funds can drop by an average of over 1 percent per year. Usually, in a year when such losses in capital occur, it will be happening during economic periods of high uncertainty and the effective rate of return reflected by interest payments during this time will be very high. During the most recent collapse of financial markets, the capital value of junk bond funds dropped dramatically, but during that time, the interest rate (or yield) was above 15 percent per year. Anyone using these funds as a source of income would be wise to limit income spending to 7.5 percent and direct that any further yield be used to buy additional shares so that capital is retained.

If fluctuations in capital value are emotionally upsetting, then you would lean more toward short-term bond funds and government guaranteed GNMA funds. For a greater annual income from bond funds, learn to live with the more volatile high-yield bond funds that will generate annual income about 2 to 3 percent higher than the other two candidates.

Chapter 16—The Danger Zone

A Critical Time Early in the Retirement Years

The three basic risks of retirement are inflation, longevity, and investment risk. This chapter explores the most fundamental challenge impacting the management of retirement assets. It highlights the problem and offers some basic strategies to combat the problem. The following chapter will go further to explain additional considerations when extracting money from retirement resources. The key message is the reminder that taking more from the fund than a combination of interest and dividends can be a big mistake. Yet the financial planning community sometimes recommends distributions of 7 percent when the expectation is a 10 percent annual rate of return.

Attention All Spendthrift Shoppers

A danger zone for retirees is the critical period for about the first seven years into retirement—typically from age sixty-six through age seventy-three. Why does this period deserve special attention? Because if our investments lose money while we are also tapping our nest egg for income, the combined result can be catastrophic. This potential double whammy can dramatically reduce what we will need to generate adequate resources in the distant future—assuming we have a distant future by living long lives.

It may sound counterintuitive, but if we have two balanced mutual funds with twenty-year periods that generate the exact same average annual rate of return, the success of one over the other can vary dramatically when each is used to fund a retirement income. While one may last to perpetuity, the other will run out of money.

The classic illustration of this problem can be found in Canadian Professor Moshe Milevski's research. He uses the example of two actual balanced mutual funds that had the same average rate of return (10.4 percent) over twenty-one years from 1985 to 2005. However, fund A had several loss years early and made it back in the end. Fund B did fine initially and then lost money at the end.

Here are the year-by-year results:

Year	Fund A	Balance		Fund B	Balance
1985	-18.39%	$100,000		17.56%	$100,000
1986	-4.59%			8.72%	
1987	-19.14%			-3.35%	
1988	18.47%			20.08%	
1989	14.30%			19.62%	
1990	6.79%			-13.64%	
1991	14.59%			17.68%	
1992	-15.40%			11.11%	
1993	8.95%			16.39%	
1994	16.57%			-9.11%	
1995	33.60%			-9.76%	
1996	16.21%			12.62%	
1997	19.52%			-16.36%	
1998	20.72%			7.72%	
1999	21.03%			36.73%	
2000	-1.61%			27.59%	
2001	21.22%			12.80%	
2002	13.92%			20.75%	
2003	5.26%			14.99%	
2004	19.61%			28.95%	
2005	26.57%	$658,000		-3.74%	$658,000

The twenty-year average rate of return for both funds happened to be identical. It was 10.4 percent.

Now, if we start to withdraw $7,000 per year from each fund, let's see what happens to the account that suffered losses during the early "danger zone" years.

Year	Fund A	Balance	Fund B	Balance
1985	-18.39%	$ 74,606	17.56%	$ 110,559
1986	-4.59%	$ 64,183	8.72%	$ 113,202
1987	-19.14%	$ 44,898	-3.35%	$ 102,406
1988	18.47%	$ 46,189	20.08%	$ 115,966
1989	14.30%	$ 45,796	19.62%	$ 131,714
1990	6.79%	$ 41,905	-13.64%	$ 106,743
1991	14.59%	$ 27,705	17.68%	$ 118,612
1992	-15.40%	$ 23,184	11.11%	$ 124,794
1993	8.95%	$ 20,026	16.39%	$ 138,246
1994	16.57%	$ 19,754	-9.11%	$ 118,654
1995	33.60%	$ 15,955	-9.76%	$ 100,069
1996	16.21%	$ 12,070	12.62%	$ 105,695
1997	19.52%	$ 7,571	-16.36%	$ 81,380
1998	20.72%	$ 2,163	7.72%	$ 80,659
1999	21.03%	$ -	36.73%	$ 103,287
2000	-1.61%	$ -	27.59%	$ 124,785
2001	21.22%	$ -	12.80%	$ 133,757
2002	13.92%	$ -	20.75%	$ 154,516
2003	5.26%	$ -	14.99%	$ 170,683
2004	19.61%	$ -	28.95%	$ 213,099
2005	26.57%	$ -	-3.74%	$ 198,139

It's not enough to wind up at retirement with what looks, on paper, to be plenty of money. We can see that there is a danger zone for retirees who start taking income from their retirement account that is not supported by enough gains. What this also illustrates is the danger in taking out more than is justified beyond just interest and dividends. The principal should remain intact.

The Bucket Brigade: Pros and Cons

Some suggest having "buckets" of different asset types and taking early money from the cash bucket. The basic idea is to leave money in stocks to protect against inflation and to avoid the possibility of taking income from a plunging stock fund. This may sound reasonable, but it doesn't work very well in practice. What happens over the first seven years or so is that too much of the cash may be gone and the asset mix will then be concentrated in stocks. That's the last place it should be for someone well into retirement by that time.

Having just pointed out the dangers of accessing income only from our cash "bucket" (or non-stock-market assets) during a downturn in the stock market, let's consider the situation where this may be our only alternative. While we may be in a period of having to pick our poisons, it can be reassuring to note that our danger zone may be short-lived. Consider once again for emphasis what we learned earlier—that the stock market, since 1974, has experienced six major crashes involving losses of more than 35 percent. In each case, the average return in the first twelve months following the market bottom was 39 percent. The second twelve-month period saw 12 percent gains. Those were just averages. In fact, the greater the downturn, the more substantial the snapback will be. Witness what has happened in the most recent crash—the worst in seventy years. After a 50 percent drop, we have had a 70 percent gain in the first twelve months following the market bottom. Four and a half years after the bottom, we are up 180 percent. The average recession has lasted just sixteen months. A little patience can go a long way for an investor who maintains some historical perspective.

Having to invade our nest egg from the cash side of our total asset mix may only be temporary. When the market recovers, we will be able to rebalance back to the fifty-fifty split that will make the most sense as a long-term allocation.

Stocks Play a Permanent Role

We can never exclude stocks because we have inflation and longevity to consider. A sixty-five-year-old woman has a life expectancy of eighty-six (eighty-three for a male.) The other half of us not dead by then may be living a lot longer. My father is ninety-eight and still going strong. Since stocks in general have outpaced inflation by a full 7 percent per year over some 150 years, we know we have to depend on this investment category to protect our future buying power. Recognizing how volatile the stock market can be, we just have to be prepared with a strategy that will provide adequate income during the inevitable downturns.

Watch Out for Annuities

Without a strategy, those reasonably certain to become octogenarians could be tempted to buy an annuity that would guarantee a lifetime income.

Playing to the fear of outliving assets, annuity sales organizations aggressively market these financial instruments, but here's the rub: at 4 percent inflation, an annuity paying $1,000 per month today will be paying the equivalent of $456 in twenty years. We might just as well have lost over half of our money. If this wasn't bad enough, longevity is increasing at a rate of three months per year! In twenty years, this could mean five more years of average longevity and a further reduction in the value of our original $1,000. Using an actual example offered today, we see that in return for a $100,000 investment at age sixty-five, the annual income for life will be $7,500. In twenty years, inflation will have reduced this amount to effectively $3,400. Meanwhile, the minute this annuitant dies, the entire $100,000 is gone (kept by the insurance company), even if the annuitant dies a few days after writing the check for the $100,000.

Another annuity/life insurance pitch to avoid is the so-called variable annuity that ties gains to those of the overall stock market and will guarantee a minimum gain of 1 percent—even in years when the market loses money. At the same time, however, it caps gains at 17 percent regardless of how well the market does. Using this approach, the average annual return from 1991 to 2005 was 9.6 percent. This may sound reasonable until we recognize that a balanced fund (holding equal amounts of stocks and bonds) would have earned an average of 13 percent over the same period.

How much was the 1 percent guarantee worth? Well, a balanced fund like Vanguard Wellesley Income over forty years has only lost money in six of those years. Five of the losses were less than 5 percent, and the single largest lost (in 2008) was 9.8 percent followed by a 16 percent gain in 2009. The lesson here is that easily spooked retirees often pay a high price to avoid losing any money whatsoever, even if the loss would correct itself within a short period. This explains why marketing of these guaranteed investments have been so successful—and so lucrative. The hidden cost is the opportunity cost of the higher gains that could have been enjoyed in return for enduring a small number of minor periodic losses.

Coming to terms with the danger zone is one of the most difficult issues we face in retirement. The simple answer is to spend only the interest or dividends from investments except in years when the capital has appreciated by more than the rate of inflation. Then start collecting social security as early as possible so as not to tap retirement accounts any more than necessary. Select stock investments for their dividend strength and consider combinations of bond funds that generate higher interest income even though fluctuations in capital value will occur. If the interest and dividends are all that we spend, the fluctuations in the capital values of stocks and bonds won't matter.

Upon reaching a point about seven to ten years into retirement, it will be possible to lighten up a bit and start feeling relaxed about eating into the principal or capital values of retirement savings. The following chapter will drill deeper into the choices involved in taking your money out. What we learned in this chapter is that timing can be everything.

Chapter 17—Taking Your Money Out

What to Spend First

By the time we reach retirement, there are usually seven possible resources that make up our retirement nest egg. These typically include one or more of the following:

- social security
- retirement savings plan (IRAs, 401(k) plans, and other retirement plans)
- equity in a home or vacation property
- inherited money
- savings or investment account that is *not* in a tax-deferred retirement plan
- pension plan paying a monthly income
- sale of a business interest or stock options in a public corporation

Our Basic Objective

Fundamentally, our objective in the early years of retirement is to meet our living expenses while creating the smallest possible amount of drain on our resources. Creating the greatest amount of after-tax spending money for the dollars we extract from our nest egg is the ultimate goal. Social security and pension money get tapped automatically without our having to agonize over which investments to sell. Our home-equity decision takes care of itself and is usually a by-product of some other lifestyle decision—like moving to be closer to grandchildren or deciding to downsize.

Which Type to Tap First

The big question for most people has to do with investment decisions and extraction rates from after-tax regular investments versus retirement-plan assets. As a general rule, it makes sense to first access money that is not in a retirement plan. Why? Because retirement-plan money continues to earn and compound tax free. We only have to pay taxes years later when we start nibbling away at the money to fund our retirement income needs.

By comparison, it is more difficult to generate gains in a conventional after-tax investment account. On taxable money, every successful investment that we cash in and reinvest (or spend) will trigger a tax that we will have to pay. Successful mutual funds will be sending us 1099 tax reports that tell us how much we owe in taxes on the money that they made and reinvested for us. Paying these taxes will impede our successful accumulation of assets—assets that will become more and more important as we live further into our retirement years.

We are forced to start taking so-called "minimum distributions" from IRA accounts beginning at age seventy and a half, but these are minimal and there are several alternatives introduced as part of this requirement. One way to avoid the minimum distribution is by considering a Roth conversion, but this is a major step that should not be taken without careful thought. Since Roth conversions are front and center these days, we'll tackle that consideration first.

Roth IRA Conversions

The Roth conversion allows us to pay taxes today on all or a portion of our IRA money and receive tax-free income from this money, plus what it earns in compound gains, at any point in the future. The Roth IRA escapes the required minimum distribution requirement that begins at age seventy and one half, and we can pass these benefits on to heirs.

The possibility of converting to a Roth IRA may be enticing to a small subset of retirees, but for most us, it never makes any sense. Why? Because we are writing a big check to the US government—money that disappears from our nest egg with 100 percent certainty—and there is no guarantee that this payment will produce a meaningful benefit. Once we send the check for taxes we have to pay (the cost of conversion), the question of whether we will have received a benefit or not depends on what our retirement plan earns over the coming years. This will only be worth anything meaningful if our Roth money doubles or triples in value.

We have to remember that the taxes we pay to convert to a Roth, if left in our portfolio of investments, would also have gained in value as well. Plus we would have maintained control of a greater amount of money instead of sending a big check off to the government. All Roth conversion discussions seem to conveniently forget that, by not paying the substantial conversion tax cost, we otherwise would have had that tax money continuing to grow if left alone in our mutual-fund accounts. This money, including what it earns over the years, could amount to more than enough to pay whatever taxes the Roth conversion was intended to avoid. In the meantime, we had complete control over all of our money.

Marginal Tax Brackets

When taking money out of a retirement plan, we can never lose sight of what we paying in taxes on each additional amount of money that we draw. As a retired California couple with, say, $65,000 of taxable income, we probably will pay a total of about 17 percent of this amount in taxes. However, once adjusted gross income (taxable income or "AGI") reaches about $36,000 for single people (and $72,000 for married couples), the dollars we receive over that amount will be taxed (federal plus California) at 25 percent or more. As we increase our incomes by accessing retirement money or by earning more in interest on say, bank CDs, that additional income will be taxed at our highest marginal bracket. This is important to remember, because it helps to explain why we may be better off spending existing after-tax capital rather than accessing retirement money that will be coming out of the IRA as additional, highly taxed dollars over and above what we already receive from social security and other sources.

What follows is a chart that will lead to better-informed decisions about what money to take and when to take it, based on the tax impact of those decisions.

Personal Tax Worksheet

A critical step toward a full knowledge of retirement finance is to gain an understanding of how the government taxes your income. Generally speaking, you don't pay much in taxes on the first half of your income. Instead, the government chooses to really "sock it to you" on the last half of what you receive. It is the "progressive tax rate," or the practice of taxing at an ever-increasing percentage as income goes up. The following schedule will help you calculate the tax rate on each additional dollar you receive in income. These tax percentages are known as your marginal tax rates because they illustrate the rate that you pay at the outer limit of your income.

Approximate "Marginal" Income Tax Percentages
(percent tax on the last dollars of income)

Includes Both Federal and California State Taxes

Single Persons		Married Persons *	
Taxable Income	**% Tax**	**Taxable Income**	**% Tax**
$8,925 to $36,250	18%	$17,850 to $72,500	20%
$36,250 to $87,850	33%	$72,500 to $146,400	33%
$87,850 to $183,250	37%	$146,400 to $223,050	37%

*If your spouse is also working, use your combined incomes to estimate your marginal income tax brackets.

**Remember for each exemption you claim, subtract $3,900 from your gross income and also subtract the standard deduction or itemized deductions to determine your taxable income.

Taxes Impact All Financial Decisions
Marginal tax rates have a major impact on financial decisions retirees have to make. Some couples may consider having one spouse go back to work part-time to generate additional income. If a new part-time job raises their taxable income (AGI) from say $65,000 up to $90,000, how much will disappear in taxes?

The Personal Tax Worksheet shows that what looked like an additional $25,000 will fall mostly in the income band where the combined state and federal tax rate is at least 33 percent.

Example
Assume a couple's adjusted gross income after deductions and exemptions is $72,500 (the low point of one of the above tax bands.) The proposed part-time job pays exactly $24,000 and falls into the 33 percent band—for a tax of almost $8,000. Adding social security and Medicare of almost 8 percent brings the total marginal tax to 41 percent.

This amounts to a 41 percent tax on the additional family income from part-time work. The lesson here is that we shouldn't waste time on a job interview without first reviewing the tax arithmetic of the possible after-tax income weighed against commuting costs and lifestyle considerations.

Adjustment in lifestyle and reduced spending may turn out to be more satisfying than the limited after-tax rewards that a job commitment might bring.

This illustration analysis of the high tax on the last dollars of income also applies to money distributed from a retirement plan as additional taxable income and explains why it makes sense to tap after-tax savings first to fund retirement spending needs.

The Safe Haven of Self-Employment

For the self-employed (small business owners or those working as independent contractors), the situation is truly dire, because they pay both halves (employee and employer share) of social taxes, *but* the saving grace is that they have a business that offers opportunities for tax write-offs. In a small business setting, there are many expenses that are a normal part of life's experience that can be treated as necessary business expenses. An accountant would say that you only need a "toehold of rationale …" Hobby businesses can even lose money for extended periods of time, which makes the cost of a hobby effectively tax-deductible.

At stores like Staples and Office Max, the busiest times are now in the evenings. This is when people who have kept their day jobs are buying supplies for the businesses they operate from home in their spare time. It is a growing national statistic.

Required Minimum Distributions

The reason the government insists on having retirees take money out of retirement plans is because the intent of the law was never one of providing a means of passing a retirement account on to heirs. The generous tax benefits during the accumulation stage were offered for a sole reason—to help people provide, on their own, for an adequate and comfortable retirement. This explains why the government insists that we start taking money when we reach age seventy and one half.

Making required minimum distributions from a retirement plan can be complicated—depending for openers on whether or not someone is dead or alive by what otherwise might have been their RBD (required beginning date). Different rules apply for heirs if someone dies before age seventy and one half or if they die after they have started taking money. The rules and calculations are different for retirees whose spouses are younger but within ten years of the retiree's age and the spouse is more than ten years younger. For heirs other than spouses who inherit an IRA or other retirement plan, it can be much more complicated. The money from a retirement plan is subject both to income *and* an estate tax if an estate is large enough so that the latter applies.

Suffice it to say that there are many, many issues that arise when it comes to making informed decisions on the issue of retirement-plan distributions. The best book on the subject is titled *IRAs, 401(k)s and Other Retirement Plans—Taking Your Money Out* written by Twila Slesnick and John C. Suttle. It is by far the most comprehensive and readable book on the subject; everyone with a retirement account should own a copy.

It is important to recognize that required distributions are not that onerous. At age seventy and a half, you're expected to take out about 3.5 percent of our money per year. By age eighty, the minimum is about 5.5 percent. These are amounts of money we would be earning in interest and dividends anyway. Nobody is forcing us to invade the principal until about age ninety. The penalty for not making a RMD is 50 percent of the amount that should have been paid out. That should be enough to get anyone's attention on this matter.

When it comes to spending our retirement money, we set the stage by dividing our assets between bond and stock mutual funds—the latter investing in stocks that pay dividends. To the extent that we have after-tax, non-retirement-plan assets, we should access those first or draw income from them. If we have to invade the nest egg, the money should come from this resource on which we have long since paid taxes.

If the stock-market collapses, we should not access our stock-market assets by any more than just the dividends that are paid out. Instead, we should look to our bond fund "bucket" spending both the interest and as little of the principle as our lifestyle will tolerate.

Forget the Roth, unless you have more money than you know what to do with and are determined to leave as much as possible to your children and grandchildren.

Do some homework with respect to your choices regarding the required minimum distribution.

Don't take a job just for money without calculating the after-tax take-home pay.

Chapter 18—Using a Financial Planner

Pay for advice or do-it-ourselves.

Plan the Work; Work the Plan

Financial planners can play a valuable role in helping the average retiree sort through the various issues included in the big picture of retirement finance. However, these professionals come with a cost, and this is one area where you don't always get what you pay for. The conflicts in the financial-services industry are the subject of current legislation to try to define, once and for all, what rules should apply to brokers selling investment product versus advisors who charge a fee and do not sell product. More complicated still are the professionals who represent the middle ground in that they charge a fee but offset that charge by any commission income they receive. The selection of advisor types boils down to the following spectrum: a traditional broker who gets paid commissions for selling stocks or mutual funds; fee-based advisors who will charge a specific fee but who will offset the fee if some of what he or she recommends happens to pay a commission; a fee-based advisor charging a fee based upon the size of your account (typically 1 percent); and finally, a fee-based advisor assisting on an hourly fee basis.

Do You Need a Fiduciary or Just a Broker?

A defining element of quality centers on whether the advisor is deemed to be a fiduciary under the law. A fiduciary makes all investment recommendations in the sole interest of his or her client. They are legally obligated to do this and can be sued if they are later shown to have given self-serving advice. Fee-only investment advisors, we could argue, can represent themselves as fiduciaries because they are either charging a flat hourly fee for advice or they are billing for their services based upon some percent of assets. They benefit only to the extent that the client benefits. A broker, by comparison, is selling investments and is only held to offering those that meet the industry's "suitability standards." There are many disputes between customers and their brokers, and nobody can argue that the system is not fraught with conflicts of interest. Investments suitable for someone in today's market conditions can turn out to be totally unsuitable a year later.

Meanwhile, a retiree demanding higher returns who said they could handle additional risk is later shocked that his or her broker put them into something that could have dropped in value so precipitously. The worst example of brokerage firm products are the so-called "wrap accounts" that charge three full percentage points per year for managing an account. That huge annual expense is supposed to cover all trading costs and money management fees of what is supposedly a money-management firm selecting stocks for the account. As bad as these accounts are, aggressive marketing has allowed them to attract billions of dollars even though, after the excessive fee, they have little hope of providing acceptable returns or even much net income given today's interest rates.

A Financial Planner Can Be a Fiduciary or a Broker, but Not Both

Assuming that they have adequate experience and educational background, financial planners create value primarily on the after-tax money their clients bring to them. This is not tax-sheltered retirement-plan money but rather the money that someone has accumulated through the sale of a home or business, an inheritance, or a successful investment account that they have accumulated over the years. This money deserves a collaborative effort with an experienced professional in many cases, because any investment decision will trigger a tax (or tax loss) that will have to be taken into consideration to determine if the trade is a wise move. Retirement-plan money, by comparison, is tax insensitive. You can trade your retirement accounts all day long and never trigger a taxable event.

Because taxable or after-tax money is exposed to taxation, many people are reluctant to make investment changes that might otherwise have been constructive. There is a greater status quo bias with this money. A financial advisor as a true partner (a fiduciary) can help the investor overcome that aspect of what is now known as behavioral finance. It's the inclination of normal people to feel much worse about making a decision that leads to a loss than the same amount of anguish they might have experienced from a loss that resulted from doing nothing. For this reason, an advisor can add to the level of rational thinking that should improve results over time.

Finally, if you do hire an advisor, don't expect too much of him or her. The average tenure of a client/advisor relationship is only three years, which is about one market cycle—just long enough for an advisor to fall short of inflated expectations.

Hopefully, if you choose to work with anyone, it will prove to be a long-term relationship. When it comes to stocks, or stock mutual funds, it's important to remember that 70 percent of a stock's performance is a function of what the entire stock market is doing at the time. It's therefore questionable as to how much value an advisor can bring. No advisors have ever beaten the market. If they had that ability, they certainly wouldn't need to be working for you. So be especially wary of anyone who claims to have the ability to "time the market," because those people have proven to be perennial losers if not disasters. When the stock market is roaring upward, don't expect your conservative financial advisor's recommendations to keep pace. When the market tanks, heed the advice to stay the course. Don't blame your advisor for not advising you to cash out. If someone implied that they would time the market, you should have known not to hire them in the first place.

Doing It Ourselves, with Online Help

With the advent of the Internet, there are a variety of tools that anyone can use to get a sense of what the future holds for them. One of the most comprehensive and easiest to access is at www.troweprice.com. At its home page, you can click on a retirement planner and it will walk you through a short questionnaire that leads to a simulation of what your retirement benefit will be. In other words, it tells you when you might run out of money.

What makes this reasonably sophisticated is that it includes a Monte Carlo simulation to arrive at a calculated outcome. A Monte Carlo simulation employs a computerized database of about 1,500 possible economic factors working together both for and against each other. The outcome is based on the combined probability of all factors applied to your money invested in the combination of stocks and bonds that you have chosen. If you decide to go it alone, it would be wise to use the resources at this website.

Another possibility is a planning product at www.torridtechnologies.com, which is a more comprehensive planning tool at a nominal cost. This tool allows you more flexibility in terms of the assets you can allow to be considered, but it does not perform the Monte Carlo simulation. The combination of both tools would be the best option for more compulsive retirees.

At Vanguard (www.vanguard.com), there are several levels of planning assistance that can be free if you have certain six-figure account balances with the fund family. Those balances can include not just yours but other family members as well. Beyond the free services, for anyone with $500,000 or more, Vanguard also offers a full-blown financial planning service with costs spelled out as 0.75 percent for the first million, 0.35 percent for the second million, and 0.20 percent thereafter. This fee structure, by the way, is a good standard of comparison for anyone inclined to work with a fee-only financial advisor.

Stick to the basics and you won't need outside advice

Diversification between stocks and bonds using mutual funds that are cost effective to own is all anyone really needs to be successful as an investor in his or her retirement years. Diversification achieved by a mix of different types of stock mutual funds reduces the risk of owning stocks in general. Adding bond funds to the mix further reduces the volatility of the entire portfolio and protects against the downside in a market collapse.

The biggest mistake an investor can make is the quixotic abandonment of a long-term strategy— better known as "panic." Any time the market experiences a major crash, the voices of doom are convincing. "This time it's different. The economy has never seen a collapse like this." And so on. But the world economy is huge, and our country alone makes up a third of it. There is a tremendous amount of resilience thanks to the combined efforts of billions of people in large and small businesses who keep plodding along in an effort to make a living. In the course of human history, nothing has ever happened that brought it all to a halt—or even to a long-term decline.

Anyone having the nerves and discipline to stay the course when the world appears to be going to hell in a hand basket probably doesn't need a financial advisor. Doing the homework might take some time, but so what? You're retired. Meanwhile, it doesn't have to be all or nothing. An advisor relationship for the more problematic taxable investments could offer a sounding board for transactions and strategies you might be tempted to entertain. Enlisting the help of an objective third party can be worth what it costs.

As a final note, anyone with a history of emotional and impulsive behavior should probably enlist some professional financial assistance and take whatever advice they offer.

Chapter 19—Test-Driving Your Retirement

Preparing for the Inevitable

Managing the Money

Before leaving a current job, consider circling the wagons and establishing a single IRA by rounding up the collection of IRAs and 401(k) accounts from previous jobs. Moving all of the money into a single account will jump-start the process of managing the money effectively. It will also provide an opportunity to begin a relationship with one of the two best candidates (Vanguard or Fidelity) for managing all of your money into the future. Both institutions also offer free financial advice for accounts beyond a certain size (a few hundred thousand dollars or more), so moving everything to one place can open a window to unbiased, cost-effective information. The primary reason for setting up this account, however, is to gain a comfort level with the website, the people at the 800 number, and the money-movement process of transferring funds and setting up accounts.

The biggest challenge in retirement is psychological. It may sound great to know that you are moving on in life, but when a spouse starts asking over the breakfast table, "Do you have any place to go today?" the effect on morale can be debilitating. A successful transition into retirement is akin to pounding the beach with mortar fire before the troops start landing. Work to develop plenty of outside interests and non-work-related relationships *before* you leave a long-term job or profession.

Shorter Hours at Your Current Job

See if your current employer will consider part-time or more flexible work hours as you slide into retirement. Most employers coming out of a recession would prefer to hire or keep part-time seasoned employees—known quantities—rather than face the prospect of hiring (and firing) the revolving door of new hires. Think about how you spend Saturdays and Sundays today and imagine what life will be like when every day is like a weekend. For many, the prospect is not one of joy, because the novelty wears off quickly.

Good Health Is the Key to Retirement Success

A major objective in retirement should be to clean up any bad health habits and embark on a specific campaign to develop an improved physical condition. Start now as part of the retirement test-drive. The most inspirational book in this respect is *Younger Next Year—A Guide to Living Like 50 until You're 80 and Beyond* by Chris Crowley and Henry Lodge, MD. Another winner is *Body for the Ages: From Heart Surgery to Bodybuilding Champion* by San Francisco's Pax Beale.

A recent study determined that for a certain type of heart problem, a lifestyle change can generate the same result as open-heart surgery. Fifty percent of the subjects elected open-heart surgery, which tells us how difficult it can be for people to consider a change in the unhealthy lifestyles. Don't let one of those people be you. You will cost the rest of us a lot of money, and you might become one of the ninety-nine thousand people who die each year of hospital-contracted infections.

Money Really Doesn't Buy Happiness

What follows are some thoughts on happiness written by David Brooks, a columnist for the *New York Times*. Citing a variety of studies, he says that once basic needs are met, more money doesn't necessarily lead to a happier life. According to various studies, the daily activities most associated with happiness are sex, socializing after work, and having dinner with others. The daily activity most injurious to happiness is commuting.

Joining a group that meets only once a month can contribute more to happiness than doubling your income. Being married produces a psychic gain equivalent to $100,000 a year, according to one study. So what we can infer from this is that many people contemplating retirement may be focusing on the wrong things. They overestimate the extent to which money will improve their retired lives. If we're not careful, we can become obsessed with what we can count rather than by what will really matter.

Retirement offers a fabulous opportunity for reinvention. At least half of us in our sixties today have a life expectancy of another thirty years.

We can set our financial affairs on automatic pilot using the guidelines in this booklet and enjoy what really matters.

Suggested Reading

Common Sense on Mutual Funds, by John Bogle (founder of Vanguard Funds)

John Bogle on Investing, by John Bogle

Asset Allocation: Balancing Financial Risk, by Roger C. Gibson

A Random Walk down Wall Street: The Time-Tested Strategy for Successful Investing, by Burton G. Malkiel

Debunkery: Learn It, Do It, and Profit from It: Seeing through Wall Street's Money-Killing Myths, by Ken Fisher

Where Are the Customers' Yachts? A Good Hard Look at Wall Street, by Fred Schwed Jr.

Do You Want to Make Money or Would You Rather Fool Around? by John D. Spooner

Your Money & Your Brain: How the New Science of Neuroeconomics Can Help Make You Rich, by Jason Zweig

IRAs, 401(k)s and Other Retirement Plans: Taking Your Money Out, by Twila Slesnick and John Suttle

About the Author

Stephen J. Butler is the founder and CEO of Pension Dynamics Corporation, which specializes in the design, operation, and advisory needs of qualified retirement plans for companies in Northern California. He formed the company in 1979 and has operated more than one thousand retirement plans comprised of several billion dollars over the thirty-five year period.

Mr. Butler has written two books. The first is titled *The Decision-Maker's Guide to 401(k) Plans*, and the sequel is *401(k) Today*. After writing a cover article in *Money* magazine titled "Beware 401(k) Rip-Off," as well as other articles appearing in the *New York Times* and the *Wall Street Journal*, he is considered a national authority on the subject of hidden costs in retirement plans. Mr. Butler has testified twice in Washington, DC, once before the Department of Labor and more recently before the House of Representatives' Committee on Education and Labor. The latter testimony led to federal laws enacted in 2012 that required disclosure of all hidden costs in retirement plans.

For sixteen years, Mr. Butler also has been writing a weekly column—"Steve Butler Retirement Planner"—for the Bay Area Newsgroup Corporation. This media conglomerate includes several major newspapers, including the *Oakland Tribune*, the *San Jose Mercury News,* the *Contra Costa Times,* and roughly fifteen other media outlets serving smaller cities in the area. His weekly columns have been widely praised for clarity, education, and entertainment. Considering their subject matter, his over 850 columns to date have been said to be surprisingly pleasant to read.

Mr. Butler is a graduate of Harvard, class of '66, and attended the University of California School of Business from '66–'68. He served as an officer in the U.S. Army Medical Services Corps during the Vietnam Era. He is married to Frances Butler, a retired psychiatric social worker, and has two adult children and one grandchild. His son Mason is a veterinarian, and his daughter Elsa is a journalist. He lives with his wife and two Australian shepherds in Lafayette, California, where he enjoys golf, sailing, skiing, running, motorcycling and playing the bass violin in a jazz trio.

Open Book Editions
A Berrett-Koehler Partner

Open Book Editions is a joint venture between Berrett-Koehler Publishers and Author Solutions, the market leader in self-publishing. There are many more aspiring authors who share Berrett-Koehler's mission than we can sustainably publish. To serve these authors, Open Book Editions offers a comprehensive self-publishing opportunity.

A Shared Mission
Open Book Editions welcomes authors who share the Berrett-Koehler mission—Creating a World That Works for All. We believe that to truly create a better world, action is needed at all levels—individual, organizational, and societal. At the individual level, our publications help people align their lives with their values and with their aspirations for a better world. At the organizational level, we promote progressive leadership and management practices, socially responsible approaches to business, and humane and effective organizations. At the societal level, we publish content that advances social and economic justice, shared prosperity, sustainability, and new solutions to national and global issues.

Open Book Editions represents a new way to further the BK mission and expand our community. We look forward to helping more authors challenge conventional thinking, introduce new ideas, and foster positive change.

For more information, see the Open Book Editions website: http://www.iuniverse.com/Packages /OpenBookEditions.aspx

Join the BK Community! See exclusive author videos, join discussion groups, find out about upcoming events, read author blogs, and much more! http://bkcommunity.com/

Made in the USA
San Bernardino, CA
26 July 2016